LIGHTNING

English Electric/BAC
LIGHTNING

Bryan Philpott

PSL Patrick Stephens, Wellingborough

Frontispiece *A F 3 of 2T Squadron of No 226 OCU*
(Peter March).
Front endpaper *A F 1 of No 74 Squadron on reheat tests
at Warton* (BAe).
Rear endpaper *Built as a T 4, XM967 was modified to
T 5 configuration for development work* (BAe).

Dedicated to A.R.F.

First published in 1984

British Library Cataloguing in Publication Data

Philpott, Bryan
  English electric/BAC Lightning.
  1. Lightning (Fighter planes)
  I. Title
  623.74'64   UG1242.F5

  ISBN 0-85059-687-4

*Patrick Stephens Limited is part of the
Thorsons Publishing Group.*

Photoset in 10 on 11 pt and 9 on 10 pt Plantin by MJL
Typesetting, Hitchin, Herts. Printed in Great Britain on
115 gsm Fineblade coated cartridge, and bound, by The
Garden City Press, Letchworth, Herts, for the publishers,
Patrick Stephens Limited, Denington Estate,
Wellingborough, Northants, NN8 2QD, England.

Contents

Foreword

Throughout the short history of aviation it has been apparent that while each new decade has brought progressive advances in capability and performance, at less frequent intervals major breakthroughs in design thinking have created some giant steps forward. In recent years, the brilliant Concorde has more than doubled the speed of airliners and the Space Shuttle has demonstrated that an airliner-sized aeroplane can be rocketted into space orbit and then returned under what is ultimately conventional airborne control to a runway landing, positively pointing the way to a wide range of practical combined air-and-space craft for the future. Before all this happened, but a vital stepping-stone towards it, the understanding and establishing of safe supersonic flight was brought about in the 1950s by parallel programmes in America, France and Britain.

The Lightning was the first truly supersonic British aeroplane and went on quickly to become the first to achieve twice the speed of sound. On entry into service with the Royal Air Force not only did it double the performance of the fighter defence of this country, but it also soon began to show other exceptional qualities.

The fighter pilots found that, despite this quantum jump in performance and in the complexity of their all-weather, radar-interception task, their new fighter was no more difficult to fly than their previous equipment and was in fact more precise, accurate and delightful to control than anything before it.

This quality, which was no surprise to the makers who had deliberately aimed at a totally new standard of controllability to ensure that this potent new defence weapon would be an entirely practical operating proposition, was to become one of the hallmarks of the Lightning over a quarter of a century of successful service; and in the mid-1980s a 'tour' on Lightnings was still as much sought after by enthusiastic young fighter pilots as it had been by their fathers.

In this very well-researched book, Bryan Philpott has brought together all the main facets of the evolution and operation of one of the world's finest fighter aircraft, a fighter which, with better judgement and resolution from successive governments, could well have been developed into a second-generation defence system for the RAF. The Lightning was an aircraft with the potential for world-wide export success, whose development could have eliminated the vast cost implications and the enormous loss to UK industrial strength resulting from a continuing policy of foreign purchase for defence equipment. But that was not to be and the Lightning, now approaching the end of its useful life, remains an outstanding example of the potential of British world leadership in aviation technology if supported by the government of the day.

The author's research has been very successful and in particular the brief details in the appendices of every Lightning built will be of value to the enthusiasts. This excellent book will certainly become a standard reference work.

Roland Beamont, January 1984

Introduction

The Lightning is the only British-designed and built fighter capable of reaching speeds in excess of Mach 2 to serve with the Royal Air Force. It evolved at a time when British aviation still led the world and it suffered at the hands of politicians in the same way as the industry that created it. There is no doubt that the Lightning will go down as a classic British fighter, quite rightly taking its place alongside such aircraft as the Camel, SE 5a, Bulldog, Gladiator, Spitfire, Hurricane, Meteor, Vampire and Hunter.

It is now thirty years since the P 1 from which the Lightning was derived made its maiden flight and nearly a quarter of a century since the aircraft first wore RAF colours. The soundness of its design can be judged by the fact that it still fills a vital role in the air defence of the UK, is still a joy to fly and still thrills the crowds at air displays.

Having been privileged to be part of the organising committee of the world's biggest military air display, the International Air Tattoo (IAT), I am in a position to know that the aircraft most sought after by the public are the Vulcan and Lightning. Hardly is the ink dry on the posters that announce the dates of the IAT, before 'phone enquiries, as to whether or not a Vulcan and Lightning will be taking part, start flooding in. At the show, Lightning pilots have shown their prowess by winning many of the trophies competed for.

In 1983, the Embassy Trophy for solo jet aerobatics was won by a Lightning pilot from the LTF Binbrook, flying an F 3 aircraft which had made its maiden flight from Samlesbury on May 8 1964. On Monday July 25 when the aircraft departed from Greenham Common, the three Lightnings did a characteristic reheat climb into a blue sky dotted with fluffy clouds; they did not return for a fly past, but headed straight off to Binbrook almost, it seemed, without a backward glance. The clicking of camera shutters as they left, sounded like a thousand crickets mourning a departing friend. Were they recording the last appearance of the 'Frightening' as it is called by some, at a public air display? I rather think not, because since it first entered RAF service its planned ten-year life, which was first stretched to the mid-1970s and has now entered the 80s, seems to go on. There is plenty of life and fire in the old dog yet. . . and I, like many other aviation enthusiasts, hope that someone somewhere will have the foresight to keep a unique British aircraft in flying condition, with enough engine and airframe hours available, to keep air-show crowds happy for many many years to come.

Bryan Philpott
Newbury, February 1984

Acknowledgements

The writing of this book has been a mixture of pleasure, frustration and disappointment. Fortunately the greatest ingredient has been pleasure, created mainly by the willing cooperation of many people and organisations. Frustration has come mainly from sources where one would expect efficiency, but only experienced apathy. Letters went unanswered, telephone calls were not acted on and promises not kept. Bureaucracy and petty officialdom created problems that at times made me wonder if the Lightning is still so secret that one runs the risk of being confined to the Tower if the payload is quoted!

I am particularly grateful to Arthur Reed, who kindly allowed me to base some of my work on his own book about the Lightning, which is published in the *Modern Combat Aircraft* series. That book goes much deeper into some aspects than my own work and is therefore vital complementary reading. The British Aerospace PLC Aircraft Group at Warton were of considerable help, but then withdrew some vital papers they had loaned to me, but I should like to record my thanks to them, in particular to David Kamyia, Derek Haworth, Geoff Bartley and Rob Brockie, who kindly made his own personal Lightning records available to me. The Air Historical Branch under the direction of Air Commodore Henry Probert were particularly helpful and co-operative, as was Steve Fabian-Jones, of HQ Strike Command, who came to my rescue when I had begun to believe that RAF Binbrook was purely a figment of my imagination. Group Captain Barcilon, the station commander at Binbrook, made me particularly welcome, as did the personnel of No 11 Squadron, in particular Wing Commander John Spencer, Squadron Leader John Danning and Flight Lieutenant R. Bees. I am also most grateful to Squadron Leader Mike Weaver-Smith who could no doubt have been much more gainfully employed than acting as my escort, but he took me wherever I wanted to go and arranged answers to all my questions. I also offer my sincere thanks to Wing Commander Geoff Brindle of No 56 Squadron, who agreed to contribute the section on handling and displaying the Lightning, and then had to put up with my constant nagging until he had completed it.

In addition to these bodies, officials and officers, I should also like to record my thanks to Peter March, Richard Leask Ward, Roger Lindsay, Martin Horseman, Mike Gething and Alan W. Hall, who kindly allowed me to use material first published in *Aviation News*, the Editor of *Flight International*, for the same reasons, and to Paul Bowen of the International Air Tattoo who kindly arranged for me to meet Wing Commander Roland Beamont and to the latter for reading the manuscript and contributing the Foreword.

Articles on the Lightning have been appearing in aviation magazines for the last thirty years. I have used many of these as a base on which to start research and would therefore like to duly acknowledge my main sources, namely, *Air Pictorial, Aeroplane Monthly, Aerospace* (the journal of the Royal Aeronautical Society), *Air International, Profile Publications, Sunday Telegraph Magazine, Aviation News, Scale Aircraft Modelling, Scale Models* and *Flug Revue*. Many enthusiasts have passed information, leads, photographs and other odds and ends connected with the Lightning to me; to these and the people named and those whom I may have omitted, I would simply like to say thank you for your help, which I hope you will consider to have been time well spent.

Chapter 1

Concept and design problems

In February 1938, a Hawker Hurricane piloted by Sqn Ldr John Gillan, the commanding officer of No 111 Squadron, flew from Turnhouse in Scotland to Northolt at an average speed of just over 408 mph. This feat captured the imagination of the British public, which had heard much of the new eight-gun monoplane fighter, part of the expansion programme of the RAF, that was to replace the biplanes which had reigned supreme since the days of the 1914–18 war. In fact the Hurricane, which had started to equip No 111 squadron in November 1937, was the first RAF fighter capable of speeds over 300 mph and, three years later, was to carry the brunt of the Battle of Britain in which it shared victory with its illustrious contemporary, the Spitfire.

Whilst the RAF started to get used to the new dimensions of speed and altitude offered by the Hurricane, the expansion programme continued and, in the same year as Gillan's dash from Scotland to London, a small company received a contract to construct 75 Handley Page Hampden bombers. This company was the English Electric Company, which had been formed in 1918 by the amalgamation of five Midland engineering firms and had made a brief excursion into aeronautical engineering between 1918 and 1926. Four years later English Electric had completed over 700 Hampdens and then went on to produce 2,145 Halifax and post-war, 1,369 Vampires; all valuable experience for a Company that was to produce Britain's first jet-propelled bomber, the Canberra, and the only totally British-designed and manufactured Mach 2 fighter to serve the Royal Air Force, the Lightning.

In 1939, as war clouds gathered over Europe and the RAF's fighter squadrons began to swap more and more of their Gladiators and Gauntlets for Hurricanes and Spitfires, English Electric established a liaison office in Preston, where a Mr W.E.W. Petter, who later designed the Canberra and laid the foundations for the Lightning, started to assemble the team that within the next ten years would be thinking in terms of the problems encountered at speeds three times that of the new Hurricane and Spitfire. But in 1939 they could hardly have been aware that their biggest problems were not to be of an aeronautical nature, but those created by a post-war government that, until 1951, appeared to be determined to sacrifice not only the British aircraft industry, but also many of its allies on the altar of pacifism and unilateral cut-backs in defence.

When peace came to Europe in May 1945, Britain and America led the world in aviation matters; in fact, in some aspects of design, Britain was far ahead of the USA.

Of the major powers involved in World War 2, only Britain and the defeated Germany had managed to put a jet-propelled aircraft into front-line service. In fact the Germans had not only introduced the twin-engined Me 262 to the Luftwaffe's Jagdgeschwadern, but had also operated the world's first jet bomber as well as the rocket-powered Me 163, which still remains the only fighter using this form of power to have seen combat. In England, the Gloster Meteor had entered service with No 616 Squadron in July 1944;

although its top speed of around 420 mph made it only marginally faster than the piston-engined Tempest, it was the stepping stone to a new era. The Meteor and Me 262 never met in combat, which is perhaps just as well, since post-war evaluation gave the German fighter a top speed of over 530 mph and better handling qualities than the British jet. By the end of hostilities both aircraft had given fair accounts of their potential as well as introducing pilots to the joys of jet flight. The Me 262 had reached a higher level of development and production, with over 1,500 machines being delivered, some of which were two-seat, radar-equipped, night-fighters engaged in the defence of Berlin during the closing months of the war.

It is interesting to reflect, that it was not until January 1951, some six years after the end of the war, that No 29 Squadron was to take delivery of the RAF's first jet-powered night-fighter. This was the Meteor NF 11, whose armament of four 20 mm cannons was not as powerful as the four nose mounted 30 mm MK 108s of the Me 262!

The main problems encountered by the Germans centred on the axial-flow compressors favoured by Junkers and BMW, which were prone to blade failure, due to vibration-caused fatigue. This type of engine enabled a much smaller frontal area to be used, but at this stage of development this advantage had to be sacrificed for reliability. The British favoured the large-diameter centrifugal compressor and as they were more advanced in the development of high-temperature materials, did not suffer such a high rate of unreliability. In the main, it is probably safe to claim that German engines were lighter and more powerful, whereas the British were very much more reliable. If it had not been for the war, perhaps these two countries would have pooled their resources and produced a supersonic fighter very much more quickly, but it could also be argued that, if it had not been for the war, development of fighters, or indeed of any type of aircraft, might not have proceeded at such a pace and entry to the jet age would have been that much delayed.

There can be little doubt that, in 1945, Britain and Germany led the world in jet-fighter design. In defeat the German research fell into the hands of the Allies and continued to be of use, but sadly the British lead was eroded to such an extent that developments of the Meteor, the first-generation jet fighter, were still RAF Fighter Command's first-line fighter until the mid-1950's, by which time other nations had passed into the supersonic age.

History is notorious for repeating itself and in 1945 Britain's lead in aeronautical technology was to be as short-lived as it had been after the Great War. The progress made in gas-turbine research and advanced metallurgy, which had provided the Americans with the basis for their jet engines and British aviation with the plans for the first jet-powered airliner that were to materialise in the Comet, could only be maintained with financial support. The days of private company finance were drawing to a close, since the sums involved in the level of research necessary could not be found in the aviation industry. The giant step into the realms of supersonic flight would be costly and far beyond the reach of what previously had been covered by private ventures.

The election of a Labour Government under Clement Attlee brought widespread cancellation of military projects and orders but, perhaps more serious, was the apparent abdication of aviation research to the Americans and the export of jet engines to the Soviet Union, with seemingly very little thought being given to the ultimate consequences of the latter action. In military aviation, Britain seemed to adopt an attitude of surviving on wartime research and achievements, with little provision for modern equipment and a pitifully inadequate research programme, especially into the realms of high-speed flight. Whilst the RAF struggled on with bombers and fighters that had in the main, seen service in World War 2, the Americans introduced their second-generation aircraft including the F 84 and F 86.

Behind the scenes, however, it was not all alarm and despondency for, whilst many in the aviation industry voiced their concern about the loss of momentum gained during the war years, they were still grappling with the research problems that were eventually to lead to such fine aircraft as the Hunter and Lightning. The former though was to enter service long after it should have and the latter was to be the one and only type of its breed conceived and built entirely in England.

In 1946, the Government decreed that manned supersonic flight was far too dangerous and cancelled the Miles M 52, which at that time was well advanced and would, without doubt, have given British aviation a substantial lead in supersonic flight or at least the performance 'envelope' approaching it.

It is interesting to note that at this time, W.E. Petter, then the chief engineer of English Electric Aviation Company Ltd, had already made preliminary sketches of what was to become the Lightning. It is also worth reflecting on the views then being expressed in contemporary aviation magazines in relation to what the popular press then called the 'Sound Barrier'. Writing in the March 1946 edition of *Air Training Corps Gazette*, the forerunner of today's *Air Pictorial*, former naval pilot R.G. Worcestor stated that 'There is nothing to indicate that a basic design for supersonic aircraft has yet been evolved; in fact there is much that points to the fact that trial and error will continue to be the keynote of development until quite late stages in research are reached.' He went on to quote German research which claimed that a sweepback of more than 18° was not worthwhile because of the adverse effect it would have on lateral stability and slow-speed handling, but he concluded by forecasting that a sweep angle of 45° might be expected and the undesirable effects accepted. He also suggested that it might be necessary to dispense with the undercarriage, putting forward the argument that an item which could weigh up to 4.5 per cent of the aircraft's gross weight, served no useful purpose during fight and, moreover, occupied space near the all-important centre of gravity, could be replaced by a jettisonable trolley as used on the Me 163. Engine power presented no problem, the author stating, 'We in Britain have a significant start in the development [of supersonic flight] because the Rolls Royce engine [presumably he was referring to the Nene] is too powerful for any frame and is not the only one which has outstripped airframe design. This means that there should be no difficulty in providing the necessary thrust to achieve supersonic speed without recourse to wicked-looking wings about the size of a kitchen table.'

Worcestor left no stone unturned—he ventured into the prone position for pilots and stated the need for a G suit, whose design, he claimed, still eluded most designers. The final conclusions of this article are well worth recording in full as they do seem to illustrate the way thoughts were going in 1946.

'It is evident that the race to produce the first supersonic aircraft has been on for some months, and 1946 may well see the first aeroplane in this class. It will have a most profound effect upon fighter design rendering all subsonic designs obsolescent, and will be the basis of research into the ultimate possibility of building such aircraft with a wider application.

'The Curtiss Corporation of America, claim to have an aircraft capable of reaching 1,400 mph, but there is no confirmation that it is pilot-driven [sic]. The first step is to decide what sort of wing and fuselage is best suited, and the strongest kind of fuselage, with or without tail, capable of standing up to the unusual loads set up when an attempt is made to force the aircraft into the region of compressibility between 600–700 mph.'

At the time this article was written, the general shape of the Miles M 52 was known to most people interested in aviation and it does look as though the author of the article quoted above had little faith in certain aspects of it, especially the wing configuration.

Work was also proceeding on the tail-less DH 108 and other subsonic tail-less aircraft, and this also seems to have affected Worcestor's thoughts.

The Miles M 52 was a revolutionary design for the period; in some ways it bore a resemblance to the Bell X-1, which was to become the first piloted aircraft to exceed the speed of sound, some 18 months after Worcestor's article appeared in print. The Bell X-1 was a rocket-powered aircraft, whereas the M 52 was to have been powered by a 17,000 bhp Power Jets three-stage gas-turbine. This engine consisted of an ordinary centrifugal jet, the hot gasses from which were directed through a turbine, which doubled as a ducted fan supplying additional air. From there, the mixture passed into an athodyd duct where more fuel was ignited giving extra thrust, before it was exhausted through the tail-pipe. It was envisaged that the aircraft would climb to 36,000 feet in one and a half minutes (the Lightning achieves 30,000 feet on a reheat climb in two minutes) and attain supersonic flight at heights in excess of 50,000 feet. The pilot was to be housed in a pressurised nose cone attached to the fuselage by a tubular structure in the centre of the annular intake ducting. The whole nose cone would be ejected by explosive charges in the event of an emergency.

The short-span, laminar-flow wings had biconvex aerofoils similar to the Bell X-1, and were extremely thin, giving the name 'Gillete Falcon' to the Miles MB 3 Falcon (*L9705*) on which they, together with the tailplanes, were flight tested. The Government's decision that manned supersonic flight was too dangerous brought this promising and advanced project to a premature end in February 1946 when it was nearing completion. It is very likely that completion of the M 52 would have established a lead for Britain over the Americans, but it was not to be and the research into supersonic flight was to be undertaken by a Vickers rocket-powered, free-flight model.

This model was carried into the air by a Mosquito and released at 36,000 ft and after it had fallen 1,000 ft its C Stoff/T Stoff liquid-powered rocket ignited and accelerated the model to supersonic speeds until the fuel was exhausted. At this point the elevator was locked over and the model crashed into the sea. During flight, acceleration, pressure and elevator settings were transmitted, enabling a picture of the problems encountered to be constructed. The elevator data was important, since control was by an automatic pilot set to give level flight and knowledge of what control movements were necessary to maintain such flight was considered to be vital information in solving some of the most difficult control problems.

This research proved to be a costly failure and was abandoned after nearly £500,000 of expenditure. Writing in *Air Reserve Gazette* in March 1948, Roy Cross summed up the feelings of a lot of the aviation world when he said, 'Piloted flight is the most satisfactory way to explore the transonic and supersonic ranges, although a great deal of risk to the pilot is entailed. However, risks have always been accepted by test pilots and their answer, anyway, is a foregone conclusion. American authorities have left it to the test pilots, and as a result are well ahead of the world in piloted research. In other spheres concerning sonic research there is no reason to suppose that Britain is behind the Americans.' His suggestion that the failure of the Vickers rockets might bring reinstatement of the M 52 was not realised.

The theorising and limited knowledge gained from German papers and research were not lost on 'Teddy' Petter who, although having as a main priority the Canberra bomber, had in 1946 made provisional sketches of a supersonic fighter. His philosophy was to keep designs strong and simple, and not go looking for trouble with radical innovations. This conservative approach is well illustrated by the Canberra, which flew some 18 months after the Boeing B 47, but still remains in service today and, in refurbished form, is much sought after by minor air forces. This superlative aircraft looked quite pedestrian and

There's life in the old dog yet . . . *Some exotic and expensive modern aircraft intercepted by Lightning pilots of No 11 Squadron, and caught where they shouldn't be . . . by the camera gun of a 25-year-old, but obviously still effective, interceptor.*

Right *French Air Force Mirage F 1, shot by Flight Lieutenant M. Hale.* **Below** *USAF F 15, shot by Squadron Leader J. Danning.* **Below right** *USAF F 15, shot by Flight Lieutenant M. Hale.* **Bottom** *USAF F 5 Aggressor, shot by Wing Commander J. Spencer.* **Bottom right** *Royal Navy Sea Harrier, shot by Flight Lieutenant M. Hale (All photos courtesy No 11 Squadron RAF).*

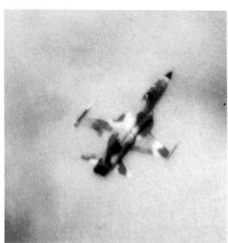

archaic beside the Boeing bomber which, in 1948, seemed to be straight from the pages of science fiction, but it outlived it and indeed served the American Air Force long after the swept-wing, six-jet B 47 had been assigned to mothballs. Petter's basic designs were therefore safe, strong and survivable, if not startlingly radical.

Petter had realised that sweep-back would be necessary to delay the onset of compressibility and that a lot of power would be needed to thrust the airframe beyond the speed of sound. A small frontal area, keeping induced drag to a minimum, was also essential, since one of the basic rules of aerodynamics is that 'drag increases as the square of the speed'. By 1946, development of British jet engines had been quite remarkable. Thus the Rolls Royce Derwent that powered the 1945 record-breaking Meteor developed 2,000 lb static thrust, against the 1946 Derwent's 3,500 lb, an astonishing rate of progress, considering that development had only started five years earlier.

Two engines would give Petter's design the thrust it needed, but housing them was another problem. The solution was to mount the power units one above the other, thus enabling the small-frontal-area rule to be successfully observed. The prone piloting position was not favoured by Petter or his chief test pilot and, in any case, presented little advantage with the engine layout he favoured. The swept wings and a conventional tailplane confirmed the designer's belief in basic aerodynamics, although at this time little was known as to the effects of sweep-back in relation to the control and handling of the aircraft. It is quite remarkable that, in June 1946, Mr Worcestor again graced the pages of *Air Training Corps Gazette*, with predictions about future interceptors, some of which were close to the eventual outcome whilst others were well wide of the mark. On this occasion he wrote that 'The short-range, very high speed aircraft will always have the most spectacular performance, and in some respects it will need the greatest skill, since the whole tempo is much quicker. There will only be fuel enough for a mission where contact with the enemy is guaranteed and the exact position of interception is planned before the aircraft is despatched. In a few years the aircraft will almost for certain be undercarriageless, and fitted with a turbine engine able to propel it at Mach 0.95.

'Although thinning the wing and sweeping it can actually prevent shock waves from compressibility, the drag of any wing at supersonic speeds is so great that the subsonic aircraft must be regarded as normal equipment for some years.

'The future interceptor then, may well be regarded as a sort of Vampire replacement, it will have an improved overall performance and land on a skid. The armament is likely to see further changes — the 20 mm gun may gradually be replaced by the 30 mm type, probably two per aircraft being the standard armament.'

Two months later in the pages of the same journal, the eminent aviation writer, Captain Norman Macmillan, also saw fit to outline the dangers facing pilots and questioned man's ability to withstand the 'dangerous belt [sic] between subsonic and supersonic speed'. He predicted that test pilots knew, all too well, the risks involved in the attainment of what he termed 'this scientific triumph' and described them as explorers who would bring a great advance in aviation in the wake of their discoveries. But just as there are sceptics today, they also existed in 1946, and Macmillan's and Worcestor's discourses on supersonic flight were challenged by C.G. Grey, who questioned what he termed '. . . the fanciful popular daily press and their claims of jet-propelled flight at 500-600 mph in the stratosphere for 5,000 or 6,000 miles' and asked too, 'Who wants to do such things?' Admittedly his question was aimed at the prophets of future commercial air travel, which was of course to benefit from investigation into supersonic flight, and alternative power units such as the turbo-prop, but it reflected a not uncommon view of that time.

In early 1947, Petter took his proposals to the Ministry of Supply (MoS) and in May of that year — somewhat to his surprise — was awarded a study contract (ER 103) for a supersonic aircraft. The specification called for a speed of Mach 1.5 at 30,000 ft which was almost identical to that of the cancelled M 52, but it must be remembered that by this time most of the captured material on aerodynamic design carried out by the Germans had been absorbed and improvements in power plants were greatly influencing the way ahead.

On October 14 1947 Captain Charles (Chuck) Yeager of the US Air Force became the first man to fly faster than sound when he took the rocket-powered Bell X-1 to Mach 1.45 at 70,000 ft, thus capturing prestige for the American nation and answering some of the questions posed earlier, about man's ability to survive supersonic flight, if not those concerning the aerodynamics of his craft. The Bell X-1 was a sturdy machine that initially handled very badly, but was improved upon until it achieved its design objective and returned in one piece.

In Great Britain many blind turns were taken, with too much emphasis being placed on radical designs such as the DH 108. This tail-less research aircraft, which was basically a Vampire fuselage with swept wings, suffered from instability and flutter and claimed the life of Geoffrey de Havilland before the late John Derry pushed it through the sound barrier in September 1948. The DH 108 was nothing more than a test vehicle, whereas the swept-wing North American XP 86, which made its maiden flight on October 1 1947, was a firm proposal for a fighter design that was to see service in the USAF long before the RAF had anything approaching its performance. In fact the F 86 Sabre, as it was to become known, was supplied to the RAF in 1953, five years after it became the first fighter capable of supersonic speed to equip a western air force (USAF), as an interim measure to give pilots experience of flying swept-wing jets before the arrival of the Hunter.

Apart from its aerodynamic contribution the F 86 can trace another link with the Lightning, for in May 1948 Wing Commander Roland Beamont during a visit to Muroc Test Centre (now Edwards Air Force Base) dived an F 86 to Mach 1, becoming the first Englishman to reach the speed of sound. His enthusiastic report of the handling of the Sabre was well received by the English Electric design team at Warton, which had by now decided that conventional shapes were the key to a successful supersonic fighter, a view that Petter had held from the very early days.

Wing Commander Beamont was one of the leading members of the Lightning project team, he was connected with it from its inception and was responsible for the flight-testing evaluation programme from its very inception in 1948 until his last Lightning test flight twenty years later. Arthur Reed, the air correspondent of *The Times*, quite rightly observed that Petter's and his successor Freddie Page's continuous integration from the beginning of the test pilot with the design team was one of the main reasons why the P 1 and its successors always had such excellent flying characteristics, despite the barriers that had to be crossed during their development. 'Bee' Beamont must therefore be credited with his tremendous contribution to a fighter that was a real pilot's aeroplane and which could have been far more successful than it was allowed to be by the politicians.

Chapter 2

Early development and prototypes

The MoS issued their Experimental Requirement 103 (ER 103) in 1947. This was a design study for a research aircraft capable of exploring transonic and low supersonic speeds. English Electric and Fairey Aviation submitted proposals, the former being designated P 1 and the latter FD 2. The Fairey design was purely a research project, although later it did go on to capture the World Air Speed Record and, with modified wings, played an important part in the Concorde programme, as well as providing useful data for the GAM Dassault Mirage 111 fighter. English Electric's P 1 however, was designed to be built to fighter-strength factors and be capable of being developed into a practical fighter.

Petter opted for a 60° sweep on shoulder wings, the fuselage frontal area being kept to a minimum by staggering the twin engines on a common centre-line, the lower unit being mounted well forward and having a long jet-pipe. One major change was the repositioning of the tailplane, which in Petter's initial design study had been mounted on top of the fin, but was now slung low on the rear fuselage. The ER 103 design study was sufficiently impressive to lead the MoS into issuing specification F23/49, which basically broadened the requirements of ER 103 to include guns, a sighting system and fighter-type handling characteristics. This did not go out to general tender, as English Electric were awarded the contract, for two prototypes and a structural-test airframe.

In addition to the two research aircraft which were to be designated P 1A, the contract, which was signed on April 1 1950, also called for an intensive wind-tunnel-research programme. In 1947, English Electric had the foresight to look at supersonic research and not having a great deal of money available to invest in airframes, had wisely decided that a transonic/supersonic wind-tunnel would be a worthwhile investment. Consequently Dai Ellis was instrumental in obtaining some 'flying-time-expired' Nene jet engines and built them into an induced-flow wind-tunnel, which first ran at transonic speed on July 20 1950. This was the first privately owned transonic tunnel outside the USA, and one of the P 1A models which was tested in it during 1951 is now on display in the Science Museum in London. Previous research, including some of the captured wartime German records, had led to the selection of a highly swept wing and wind-tunnel tests confirmed that this configuration should give optimum supersonic performance with the power then available. The basic reasons for using sweep-back are to postpone the onset of local supersonic flow to higher transonic speed, delaying the drag rise and/or to reduce wave drag, the dominant component of drag, in supersonic flight. There are of course drawbacks, including the reduction of lift at low speeds and the need to counteract roll due to sideslip during cross-wind take-offs and landings.

Many of the early swept-wing aircraft suffered from cross-wind handling problems, due to their high rolling moment, resulting from sideslip, and the poor effectiveness of swept trailing-edge controls at high incidence. The unswept ailerons on the Lightning avoided

Above *The experimental Short SB 5 used to verify the wind-tunnel tests carried out to prove the Lightning's tailplane position and wing-sweep. In these views, WG768, has the tailplane in the low position and the wings at 60° sweep (MoS).*

this problem, which had been highlighted during the early collection of research data, when the desirability of the aileron-hinge line to be at right angles to the line of flight was shown. The values finally selected for the P 1, to avoid violent buffeting and trim changes in transonic flight, were 60° sweep on the leading edge and 52° on the trailing edge, this giving the required zero hinge-line sweep to the ailerons to make them normal to the direction of flight. The 60° sweep with its 5 per cent thickness and 0.15 taper ratio, was a unique design whose blunt leading-edge wing section, contributed to the efficiency of the wing at subsonic speeds giving the Lightning that all-important element of control right through the speed envelope. This led one contemporary journal to comment that the Lightning was a 'honey of an aeroplane, responsive and sweet to handle from ground level to operating heights, from low speeds of 130 kts to Mach 2 plus, and inherently stable over the whole speed range'. Achieving the ultimate in one direction often opens problems in another and such wa· the case with the early aerodynamic work on the P 1.

The thinness of the chosen wing-form meant that the wheels had to be of large diameter and the mid-set position of the wings led to long undercarriage legs, as it was clear that the aircraft would take-off and land at high angles of attack.

On the P 1 the main gear was designed to retract outwards, while the nose oleo folded forwards and turned on its side to lie flat under the intake ducting, and thus the initial problems posed by the wing design were fairly easily overcome. However slide-rule and wind-tunnel research, which in the late forties and early fifties involved many man-hours of calculation that today would be quickly analysed, digested and formulated by computers, was not always believed or trusted by scientists who were perhaps not as closely connected with the project concerned.

Such is the advance of modern technology that it is often overlooked (or not even considered) that thirty years ago computers were in their infancy and it is not overstressing this point to comment that the capabilities now available in a comparatively inexpensive home computer are beyond those that were available to the aerodynamicists and 'stress' men in 1949–50.

The results of the wind-tunnel tests carried out by English Electric convinced them that a low tailplane position would be necessary to give the longitudinal and low-speed handling control required. This position was superior to that originally planned, of a fin-mounted tailplane, which tests indicated would give a disastrous 'pitch-up' element. As the tailplane was moved lower, so the results became better, and it was soon evident that excellent control and stability could be obtained from a low-positioned, all-moving tailplane.

The revised layout in which the wing was moved to a shoulder position, with the upper engine to its rear, gave the tailplane the desired position well below the wing wake. The findings of English Electric were supported by tests carried out in France with the Sud Est Grognard, which had flown at speeds of up to Mach 0.9 with a similar configuration and had not encountered any aerodynamic problems.

It was not so easy, however, to convince some of the staff of the Royal Aircraft Establishment (RAE) who favoured the 'T' tail layout. Despite supporting evidence from America and France that they had arrived at the same conclusions as English Electric in relation to the low-tailplane position, the MoS decided to fund a research aircraft to prove the theoretical work already carried out. Short Brothers of Belfast were awarded a contract to produce a low-speed aircraft with variable-sweep wings and adjustable empennage, having either low- or high-set elevators. The wing sweep could be adjusted (on the ground) to give angles of 50°, 60° and 69°, and it was with the first of these that the aircraft, designated SB 5 (*WG768*), made its maiden fight on December 2 1952, in the hands of Tom Brooke-Smith. The SB 5 was not unlike the P 1 in overall shape, although initially its high-positioned tailplane, adopted on the insistence of the RAE for its first flights, gave it a rather unbalanced appearance. The aircraft proved to be difficult to fly, and it was not until a year later, in December 1953, when 60° sweep and the RAE-feared low-tailplane position were adopted, that its handling became acceptable.

It can be argued that the whole SB 5 programme was a waste of money and, indeed, there are many who are forthright in putting this point of view, but it was an interesting aerodynamic test vehicle. Although ultimately it only served to prove what had been calculated in the wind-tunnel and water-tank, it did make a valuable contribution to the Lightning development programme, as well as providing important data for other research programmes before it was withdrawn from use in 1968, allocated the serial *8005 M* and moved from its base at Bedford to Finningley for preservation.

In 1950, Petter left English Electric to move to Folland where he was responsible for the Gnat. His place was taken by Freddie Page, the chief 'stress' man on the P 1 project,

Above *The P 1 experimental aircraft, from which the Lightning was developed, lands after an early flight* (via R.L. Ward).

Below *A pleasing plan view of the P 1 showing the original straight wing* (English Electric).

who later rose to become Sir Frederick Page and chairman of British Aerospace's (BAe) aircraft group. Petter had been deeply involved in the Canberra bomber project and while he had worked from the very early days on the proposed supersonic aircraft, his work-load was mainly taken up with the twin-jet bomber. Page, who had been his deputy, found himself leading a very dedicated team and under his drive the P 1 took on a new impetus at a time when over-zealous bureaucracy could have caused it to mark time. During the building of the SB 5, work on the P 1 prototypes continued, much of it being conducted with models in the 9 ft × 7 ft wind- and 18 inch water-tunnels.

Much of the pioneering work carried out by the English Electric design team was gradually verified by the SB 5 flight programme and there must have been a terrible temptation for Warton to say 'we told you so'. However, one aspect of the programme brought forewarning of a problem involving wing design. High tip lift resulting from the complicated vortex patterns created by all highly swept and tapered wings, created some asymmetric flow break-down at low speeds, resulting in poor lateral control at slow speeds. This manifested itself in early 1954, when the SB 5 developed a tendency to rock laterally in the low-speed envelope. Wind-tunnel tests confirmed that this was caused by the irregular breakdown of airflow causing the tips to stall. Wing-fences as used on the F 86 and MiG 15, could cure this phenomenon, but there was a weight and drag penalty, so an alternative solution was sought and quickly found. Further tests in the wind-tunnel indicated that either a sharp leading edge or notches parallel to the flight line, would solve the problem. In an interview with Arthur Reed, Freddie Page recounted how his design team had studied all the information available relating to flow patterns on the tips of high-speed wings and come to the conclusion that a device tested by the Americans, and then abandoned, was the answer. This was a small leading-edge notch! Both the sharp leading-edge and the notched wing were flight tested, the latter being preferred as it did not affect induced drag in the attached-flow regime, whereas the former destroyed leading-edge suction.

The notches, which were axial cuts about six inches deep and one inch wide, stabilised

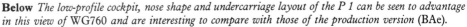

Below *The low-profile cockpit, nose shape and undercarriage layout of the P 1 can be seen to advantage in this view of WG760 and are interesting to compare with those of the production version* (BAe).

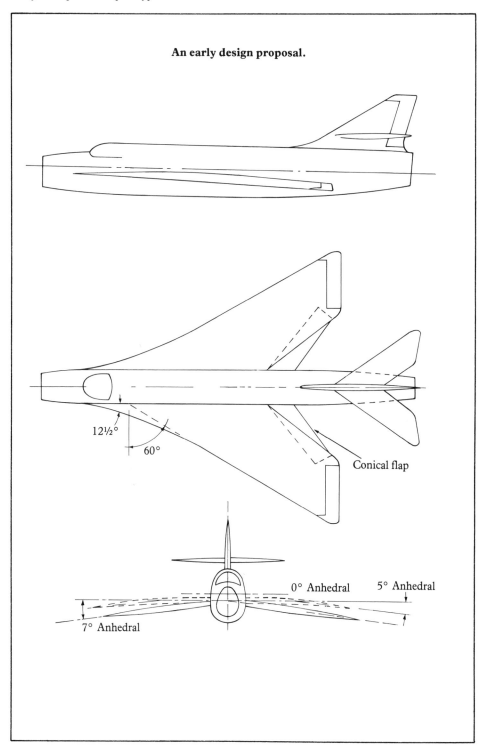

An early design proposal.

12½°

60°

Conical flap

0° Anhedral   5° Anhedral

7° Anhedral

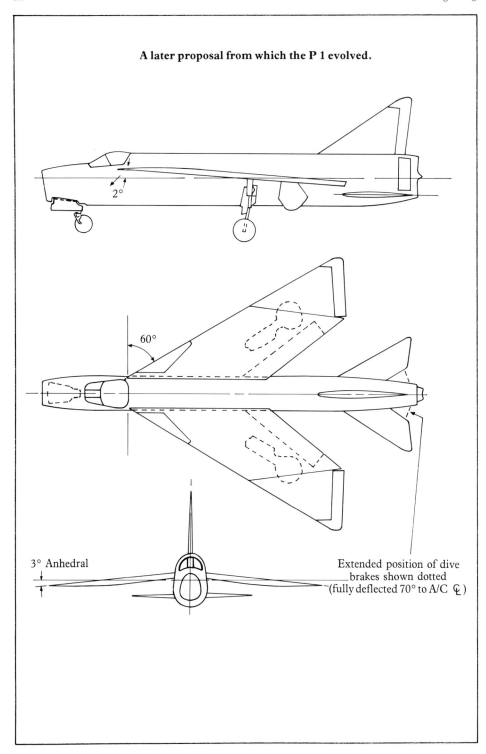

A later proposal from which the P 1 evolved.

2°

60°

3° Anhedral

Extended position of dive
brakes shown dotted
(fully deflected 70° to A/C ₵)

the airflow over the outer wing and were adopted on the P 1A for the first 95 flights. They proved to be unnecessary for low-speed flight and were progressively filled in, so that the effect of reducing the slot could be studied; this study led to the slot being reintroduced in a smaller size for transonic reasons, at a later date during development. The notches provided a useful 'quiet' zone for the wing fuel-tank pressuring-vent and were subsequently used throughout development and production. The wing configuration and low-set tailplane, tried on the SB 5 in December 1953, proved to be stable and trimmable until the wing stalled, with no 'pitch up' over the whole flight envelope — a situation that was known could not have occurred with a 'T' tail, which would have produced dangerous 'pitch up', not desirable in a combat aircraft. In transonic conditions — not explored by the SB 5 — there was a very slight trim change because of the shift in aerodynamic centre when decelerating in the region of Mach 1. Although it was subsequently discovered that some of the lateral rocking experienced with the SB 5 was accentuated by its manual ailerons, the investigation this sparked off did produce positive results in the form of the 'saw-cut' notch, which was lighter, simpler and less drag-producing than the conventional (for the period) boundary-layer fences.

Petter favoured the Rolls Royce Avon for the P 1's power units, but prior development and production commitments prevented this, so the 8,100 lb-thrust Armstrong Siddeley

Below *This view of the P 1 clearly shows the annular air-intake shape and low cockpit profile. At this time the aircraft was fitted with cambered leading-edge wings* (BAe).

Sapphire ASSa 5 was chosen. The staggered layout of the twin engined installation reduced the frontal area by 50 per cent, so in simple terms, the P 1 with a frontal area of a single-engined aircraft, had the thrust of two engines to push it into the transonic area. The Sapphires were capable of pushing the aircraft to its potential of Mach 1.12 but, above the speed of sound, their available thrust gave such poor acceleration that the aircraft would run out of fuel before it reached a limiting Mach number. Nonetheless, they proved the airframe design potential and it must be remembered that the P 1 was *not* a fighter but a research aircraft with fighter handling qualities. No armament or associated radar equipment was carried as it was primarily a prototype designed to prove that the theory of the chosen layout would be a sound base for a fighter.

The twin-engined layout enabled the aircraft to fly on one power plant without the associated asymmetric problems, a distinct advantage in the event of a power failure, since a return to base on one engine presented no major difficulties. Another plus was the recovery of the aircraft, for single-engined supersonic fighters do not have particularly good gliding characteristics and failure of the engine usually resulted — and often still does — in the pilot baling out. With two engines, the P 1 could maintain supersonic speed without the use of reheat, thus saving fuel which would be burned in enormous quantities in the case of a single-engined fighter attempting the same, but having to use reheat to do so. In fact fuel consumption was a problem on the P 1 and gave it an extremely short flight duration but, as previously stated, this was a research aircraft and the problems highlighted by it enabled solutions to be found in the development and pre-production aircraft. This same problem, of high fuel consumption, was acute for the Hunter F 1 and could no doubt have been overcome if this fighter had been subjected to the same method

Left *The second P 1, WG763. This was the aircraft displayed at Farnborough in 1955, which was fitted with guns and a 250-gal ventral tank. It is now on display in the Air & Space Museum, Manchester* (BAe).

Below left and below *Port and starboard views of the historic WG760 in store at Binbrook in October 1983. The aircraft has been completely restored and is in pristine condition* (author).

Above WG 760 *soon after its arrival at Binbrook in July 1983 from RAF Henlow* (Peter March).

of procurement, that is 20 pre-production test aircraft; as it was, it entered service with a virtually useless duration. (See *Hawker Hunter* by Francis Mason).

Another consideration which had to be taken into account was the method of introducing air to the engines. In 1950, the side intakes favoured by some designers were causing difficulties, so a nose intake which produced the greatest possible efficiency was chosen for the first two airframes, *WG760*, to be used for handling and performance development, and *WG763*, for structural research and armament investigation. The third of the initially contracted airframes, *WG765*, never flew and was retained at Warton for static tests. The mysteries of intake design, being unravelled in the early 1950s, formed just one of the problems facing all aircraft designers; another was the question of the reduction of drag by the then infant theory of area rule.

Many prototypes in the early 1950s were greatly influenced by the incorporation of area ruling, this being evident in some of the shapes coming off the drawing board, each claiming to be better than earlier models or rival companies' airframes. It has been suggested that English Electric met the requirements of the rule by accident but this is not true—this story probably emanates from the shape of the P 1 which showed no obvious attempt at fancy sculpting. The fact is that the long, parallel fuselage and sharply swept wings, required little contouring to meet the rule and actually came even closer to maximum compliance when the ventral tank was added to the second aircraft.

One of the difficulties encountered by pilots flying research aircraft at high Mach numbers, was the high forces required to operate the controls. Aircraft such as the thick-winged DH 108, whilst attempting to break new ground, placed far too much reliance on out-of-date technology, although whether or not the real importance of this was totally appreciated, at the time, by everyone concerned with such products must remain conjecture. It was not only a question of the pilot requiring tremendous strength but also of the control cables, operating the flying surfaces from the stick and rudder bar, stretching under the loads forced on them—not particularly desirable at the speeds then being attempted. English Electric had been experimenting with power-operated controls in a Halifax bomber and at an early design stage it was decided that such controls, duplicated and with artificial 'feel' built in, would be incorporated on the P 1.

Innovations like this and the high-voltage stabilised AC instead of the more customary low-voltage DC, the all-moving tailplane and the coupling of the autopilot to the instrument landing system (ILS), thus giving auto-approach, made the P 1 much more advanced than any other research aircraft with production potential then being built in the UK.

In early 1954, the Defence White Paper mentioned that a supersonic interceptor of British design would fly during that year, but the aircraft and its manufacturer were not mentioned. About this time the P 1 was taking final shape and in July 1954 it was moved to Boscombe Down for taxying trials prior to its maiden flight. Wing Commander 'Bee' Beamont carried out a total of eight taxying tests, involving 10 high-speed runs before the aircraft's first flight. These runs produced data covering nose-wheel lifting, brake temperature and the use of the braking parachute. Apart from test 5, during which the aircraft carried practically a full fuel load of 4976 lbs (= 622 galls), the rest were done with half a fuel load and an all-up weight of 25,000 lbs. English Electric Flight Test Memorandum AF/P 1/4 details the taxying tests and it is interesting to see that many of the figures previously calculated were practically spot-on. For example the report states, 'The lift-off speed on Taxi Test 3, run 1, was 125 kts at 25,000 lbs. This gives an "indicated" lift coefficient of 1.03, which agrees fairly well with the lift coefficient at the maximum ground incidence of 14.6° from wind-tunnel results. . .'

This first hop was made on July 24 1954, and served to confirm that the 'unstick' speed at 25,000 lb would be in the order of 125 kts. While the hop was extremely short, the deployment of the braking parachute was not; on this particular taxying test the 'chute was used for the second time in the series, and took 30 seconds to fully deploy, by which time the P 1's speed had been reduced to 10 kts by the wheel brakes. The report comments that in general the delay from the time the doors opened until the parachute became effective was about five seconds. The pilot's comments relating to the braking 'chute were that its opening gave a sharp nose-up change of trim and the aircraft tended to 'weathercock' quite strongly into the wind with the 'chute streamed—on one occasion full rudder was necessary to check this.

Several longer hops followed and these gave the test pilot the opportunity to assess the controls; he reported that control and stability on all three axis was satisfactory, and that the aircraft was flown off easily and landed without difficulty. The aileron response was likened to that of the SB 5 and no comment was made about any difficulty being experienced in cross-winds apart from the weathercocking mentioned above in relation to the braking 'chute. Wheel brakes operated perfectly satisfactorily apart from excessive stiffness in the pilot's hand lever and a tendency for the aircraft to skate laterally when heavily braked, especially on a wet runway. The use of the long runway at Boscombe, combined with high winds and the use of the braking parachute which made differential braking necessary, meant that fierce direct application was not needed, and throughout all the initial runs the Maxaret units were not required to operate.

Taxying and parachute-streaming trials were completed satisfactorily and the P 1 was then subjected to final, system checks prior to its first flight. The brief hops made on July 24 and 26, although enabling the pilot to get some feel of the controls, were not long enough to be considered as flights, although those who wish to be pedantic could argue that the Wright brothers initial efforts on December 17 1903 were no more than this but are classified as the world's first power flights! Prior to the P 1's maiden flight, Beamont had used a control-stimulation rig to evaluate the response and damping of the aircraft's power controls, this rig being another first for a British manufacturer.

During the morning of August 4 1954, the moment that all those connected with the project had been waiting for finally arrived. Roland Beamont taxied the aircraft to the end of the Boscombe Down's main runway, completed his pre-flight checks and set off, taking the forerunner of a rather special aeroplane into the air for the first time. The take-off run was made with flaps down and no attempt made to lift the aircraft off at its lowest calculated flying speed. The nose-wheel unstuck at 125 kts, the aircraft became airborne at 151 kts and at 160 kts the undercarriage was retracted and this last occurred with some slight asymmetry, causing a minor lateral displacement. On gradually accelerating beyond 200 kts, buffet from the flaps was noticed and at an indicated airspeed of 250 kts the flap blow-back device operated, moving the flaps to the 'up' position.

The initial handling part of the flight, during which the aircraft reached Mach 0.85, was then successfully carried out, the pilot reporting that there was no buffeting or roughness at the speed reached, his only source of embarassment being the aircraft's over-sensitivity in roll and a slight difficulty in keeping the aircraft below 400 kts during the descent. The flight was monitored by Peter Hillwood flying a Canberra 'chase' aircraft which took photographs of undercarriage operation and other aspects of the flight programme. During the final stages of the maiden flight, radio problems were encountered and Beamont experienced some difficulty with low cloud running over Boscombe, and both contributed to his abandoning a minor part of the initially planned flight test.

The undercarriage was selected 'down' at 230 kts and again there was a slight asymmetry in operation resulting in lateral displacement. The final turn to approach was made at 200 kts and the flaps were selected 'down'; the speed on the 'short finals' approach was 160 kts, when the engines were set to idle, and a normal 'hold-off' was performed with a final check at 150 kts as the boundary was crossed. A smooth touchdown at approximately 140 kts was executed and the brake 'chute was streamed at 135 kts, the latter operation on this occasion being completed within 2 secs. The parachute caused an immediate nose-up pitch together with powerful weathercocking which required a lot of correction with the rudder. So a highly satisfactory maiden flight, in which most of the predictions made during calculations on the ground were confirmed, came to an end.

The following day the P 1 made its second flight, but adverse weather conditions restricted its altitude to 1,000 ft and prevented a full flight programme from being carried out. Take-off was made at 140–150 kts, unstick occurring at 1,270 yards—as against the 1,390 yards for the maiden flight—and the undercarriage was retracted at 190 kts. Once again it was necessary to throttle back after take-off in order to keep the speed below the maximum 'flaps down' speed limitation. Turbulent air conditions beneath the cloud base made the lateral over-sensitivity more marked than it had been on the previous flight and it was also noticed that the aircraft occasionally made an erratic slow-rate rolling movement which did not appear to be necessarily connected with rough air displacement or control displacements. The landing was similar to that of the first flight, but after touch-down the attitude was kept as high as possible in order to obtain full high-drag braking forces. Wheel brakes were applied from about 100 kts, and the brake parachute was not streamed during this run.

The one flight characteristic which proved to be undesirable to the pilot was the over-sensitivity in the rolling plane. Recordings indicated that minimal corrective stick movements by the pilot were sufficient to set up a small amplitude roll, which damped out when the pilot relaxed control. The oscillation seemed to be aggravated in turbulent air conditions and became worse as the speed increased. Operation of the aircraft's under-carriage and air-brake was also likely to set up oscillation, particularly in the case of the dive brakes, which were also proving troublesome due to buffeting. The aileron movements involved were summerised from the records of the first two flights and found to be in the order of 1°–2° at a frequency of one cycle per second. A first attempt at improving the aileron characteristics was to double the jack forces to 15 lbs for full deflection for flight number three. Before the P 1's third flight, a very detailed analysis of the aileron problem was carried out that covered every aspect of the likely causes and remedies. Causes ranged from longitudinal trim resulting from the pilot holding a push force of a few pounds through much of the first two flights, to valve friction, circuit friction, circuit backlash, aileron jack-response lag and over-sensitivity. It is interesting in respect of the latter that in the 'Flight Test Memorandum' AF/P/7 covering the above-mentioned aileron-induced oscillation, reference is made to the SB 5 test programme; the gearing between stick and ailerons on the larger P 1 was between 3 and 4 times that on the SB 5, while the rolling moment per inch of stick movement fell within the same ratio. The ailerons of the SB 5 were much the same as those on the P 1 although they were not power-operated.

It is quite clear from some of the comments made that much of the work carried out by the SB 5 programme was of great use and did not necessarily serve just to prove previous theoretical tests, as has been previously claimed in accounts of the Lightning development. Whether or not it was a waste of money—another frequently made claim—as the prototype P 1s would have come up with the answers anyway, is beyond the scope of this book, but there is some evidence to suggest that, far from being a white elephant, the SB 5 played an important part in the development of supersonic flight; those involved in the project could argue points for and against it, depending on their viewpoint.

During the maiden flight of the P 1, an attempt was made to operate the dive brakes, this being at a speed of 400 kts and an altitude of 13,000 ft, but the pilot found that heavy

Below *Wing Commander R.P. Beamont brings* WG760 *close to the photographic aircraft during an early test flight* (BAe).

Above *Prototype P 1 with cambered leading-edge wing extensions and inset ailerons* (BAC).

Below *The increased area of the wing, created by the cambered leading edge, is clearly defined in this view of* WG760 (BAe).

buffeting resulted from only small movements and brought with them erratic directional characteristics. Full deflection of the dive brakes was carried out during the second flight at 250 kts, with no resulting buffet, but considerable retardation bringing a progressive nose-up trim change. At 350 kts, mild buffet occurred after the brakes were opened beyond 25 per cent of their travel and, at 400 kts, heavy buffet was accompanied by a very strong nose-up trim change which required nearly full forward stick to trim. There was also a small amount of directional and lateral oscillation at the time the brakes were fully extended. Because aileron oscillation was also present it was difficult to determine a precise cause, but of course a full investigation with respect to the aileron situation was also initiated.

The rather extensive quotations from official reports, made at the time the P 1 first flew, have not been included to highlight problems but merely to show the reader that, although the aircraft did perform more or less as was predicted, the complexity of the undertaking was bound to bring minor airframe and aerodynamic problems, and also show how these were analysed not only by the pilot's verbal reports but also flight-test recorders. It is very easy to compare modern techniques with those of only a few years ago and dismiss the latter as being primitive, but it should always be remembered that every case is relative. In the early days of flying, a note-book, strapped to the pilot's knee, and a pencil, were the best available means of recording test-flight data and served their purpose adequately. As each level of technological advance is reached it brings progress, but at the time it is first introduced it must be considered the latest and best available. So, whilst in 1984, modern electronics, the micro-chip and the computer may well take a lot of the pressure off flight testing, in 1954, when the P 1 first flew, reliance was (and in fact still is) placed on the pilot's report which was carefully scrutinised alongside records from the, then modern, equipment being used. Both the P 1 prototypes provided invaluable aerodynamic experience at supersonic speeds, and made tremendous contributions to the development of control, one example being the revision of aileron and tailplane gearing to reduce sensitivity, the early stages of the revelation of this need, being shown in the quoted reports.

Different wing profiles were also tried out by varying the basic English Electric ASN/P1/3 section, experimenting for instance with drooped leading-edge flaps on the inner wings of *WG760*, but most of these new wing profiles were soon abandoned; one modification, however, which introduced a cambered leading-edge extension, wide-chord tips, and completely inset ailerons, brought significant benefits and was later proceeded with.

On August 11 1954, the P 1 was ready for its third flight and it was on this occasion that it became the first British aircraft to exceed Mach 1 in level flight. Just off Poole Harbour with all systems functioning correctly but still a slight trace of over-sensitivity in the lateral axis, 'Bee' Beamont opened the throttles and let the aircraft accelerate. At Mach 0.98 the aircraft showed no signs of further acceleration so, after about two minutes, the throttle settings were reduced and the aircraft descended from 30,000 ft to make a long, slow descent into Boscombe Down. The following morning it was revealed to the test pilot that analysis of the flight-recording tapes and the application of compensation for a pitot-static measuring error had revealed that the aircraft had in fact reached Mach 1.00. The pitot-shock pattern had not had time to settle and enable the Machmeter to give a true reading and had thus appeared to stick at 0.98 but, if the throttle opening had been maintained for another 30 seconds or so, the shock pattern would have settled sufficiently for the pilot to have seen the magic figure register on his instrument.

It was immediately decided that during that day's flight a longer dry-thrust run would be made. Climbing to 36,000 ft the aircraft was flown parallel to the coast, the throttle opened and Mach 0.98 came up. The Machmeter again hesitated, then jumped to Mach 1.02. There was no buffeting, no instability and the aircraft responded to all control movements. Power was reduced and there was a slight change in trim as it returned to subsonic speeds. Beamont headed back for Boscombe but could not resist letting those waiting on the ground know that he had achieved Mach unity. He chose to do this by creating the, then new, phenomenon, a sonic boom. Although at this time it was not banned, officialdom frowned upon it, especially over land, but this was a day for herald-ing achievements, so at thirty miles out, Beamont lowered the nose of the P 1 to aim it at the centre of the airfield, then increased the power until Mach 1 was again recorded and those on the ground had no doubt that they had achieved the first of their objectives.

The reliability of the aircraft enabled the flying programme to proceed at a pace that soon saw it completing its 14th flight before the end of the month. Unfortunately these flights had not accumulated the necessary ten hours required by all prototypes before they could appear at the SBAC Display at Farnborough in September, so much to the dis-appointment of those connected with the project, the aircraft was not permitted to appear. During the week of the Farnborough display the P 1 did in fact make a flyover, but this was at a height of 40,000 ft and those on the ground who saw the con-trail were probably not aware that the aircraft making it was the secret, but much-talked-about, supersonic research aircraft.

Although the first two dozen flights passed off without major incident and have since been summarised in a variety of articles as being completely trouble-free, they were not without incident. The question of aileron oscillation still existed and, on flight no 7, the stick gearing was reduced by 8 per cent which brought a marked improvement below 400 kts, but had no effect on the over-sensitivity above 430 kts. On flight no 5, the cockpit filled with grey smoke when the cold-air-unit impeller disintegrated and the same thing occurred on flight no 13. It was also noticed during the early flying programme that, in certain conditions, fuel was escaping from the leading-edge notch, particularly on the starboard side, and that there was a tendency to asymmetry in the fuel system. In the case of the latter, flight no 13 also provided useful data when, after 15 minutes, the asymmetry became particularly noticeable. On landing it was discovered that the starboard tank contained 500 lbs less fuel than the port, the loss being attributed to either an asymmetric loss through the vent, or the feeding of both engines from the tank. A thorough check was made of the whole fuel system which proved that there was no possibility that both engines could be fed from the same tank and that it was an incorrectly positioned vent that had caused negative pressure to occur over most of the flight range.

As far as the ailerons were concerned, reduction in the gearing continued to be made and by flight no 11, this had been reduced by a total of 18 per cent. The pilot's comments, after three flights with this reduction, were that it was possible to fly reasonably accurate-ly without marked over-correction in steady flight, but the over-sensitivity was still present under turbulent air conditions or during manoeuvring flight, especially in rolling at supersonic speeds.

Answers to these and other problems were found and they are not quoted to highlight any shortcomings of the aircraft. It is felt that they should be mentioned since it is quite wrong to claim that from the first flight of the P 1 until the definitive version entered service, the aircraft flew like a dream and had a trouble-free gestation — certainly the impression given by some published accounts of the aircraft's history. The problems were not as great as those experienced by some military prototypes, but they were significant enough to warrant inclusion in an attempt to put the early design, development and flights into the correct perspective. By the end of September sufficient flights had been carried out to enable the design team to conclude that they did in fact have a good platform from which to expand, and the P 1 was not in fact a 'hard-to-handle-freak' research aircraft. The way forward was to increase the power and develop the aerodynamics, the two going hand in glove since there was already some indication that above Mach 1.20 directional stability might become a problem.

In November 1955, *WG760* was fitted with a very basic reheat system which increased the available thrust from the Sapphires to 10,310 lbs, but reduced the available dry thrust by about half. This meant that in the event of an engine failure it was likely that the aircraft could not be recovered. This limitation was accepted by the test pilot who felt that if such an event occurred a controlled-energy descent was possible if properly planned. The introduction of this rather primitive form of fixed nozzle reheat enabled the aircraft to be pushed to Mach 1.5 where directional stability fell to a point where it was considered unsafe to proceed. This brought the first increase in fin area, a further three being necessary before the definitive size was achieved. Not all these changes were directly associated with an initial underestimate of the optimum design for the tail-fin, being partially due, instead, to a change of missile installation at the front end of the fuselage that affected directional stability. The second P 1, which had made its maiden flight on July 18 1955, was not fitted with the reheat Sapphires but did have a 250-gallon ventral tank and a 30 mm Aden cannon fitted either side of the cockpit. The split flaps of *WG760* were replaced on *WG763* by the more satisfactory plain, hinged type which were later adapted to carry fuel. The ventral tank was a vital necessity since limited duration was a major problem, the capacity of some 4300 lbs on the prototype giving a duration of only 55 minutes, this being highlighted in a performance summary issued in February 1955 before the aircraft was flown by selected pilots at Boscombe Down. The contemporary summary below detailed the flight envelope:

'Fuel at take-off should be about 2,150/2,150 lb, and at landing should not be less than 400/400 lb. Thus a maximum cruise at M = 0.9 at 38,000 feet would work out:

	Time	Total time	Dist	Total dist	Fuel used	Fuel remaining
	Minutes		Nautical miles			
Immediately before T/O	0	0	0	0	0/0	2,150/2,150
T/O & Climb	5	5	40	40	475/475	1,675/1,675
2 × 180° turns full power	3	8	0	40	150/150	1,525/1,525
Cruise at M = 0.9	45	53	390	430	1,075/1,075	450/450
Descent to Base	2	55	15	445	50/50	400/400

This distance and endurance could be slightly increased by cruising at M = 0.88. Use of full power at altitude more than doubles the consumption used for cruising.'

The summary went on to point out that at that time the P 1 was just supersonic in level flight, but to conserve fuel it was best to achieve Mach unity in a shallow dive. It is quite clear that the range and endurance were totally inadequate for a supersonic interceptor, which again highlights and stresses the point that the first two P 1s were not prototype fighters, but research aircraft from which a fighter could be developed. The logical development was the production of further aircraft incorporating improvements found to be needed from the first two airframes, as well as equipment needed for the interception and destruction of enemy aircraft. Development of the P 1A was only part of the original MoS contract, which also called for the construction of three operational prototypes, these being designated P 1B. During 1953, a standard of build for these three airframes was agreed and in 1954 confirmation to proceed was given.

Under the direction of Freddie Page, the design team worked on the integration of the weapons' system and its associated radar equipment into the basic airframe. The initial intention was to use a pack containing two missiles (originally Blue Jay) plus two 30 mm Aden cannons, as well as the possibility of an optional pack containing 24 FFARs (Folding-Fin Aircraft Rockets). In the end a compromise was reached, with the Adens becoming permanent installations either side of the cockpit and the missiles mounted on external pylons. The radar equipment was to be Ferranti AI-23 Airpass fire-control system.

The most extensive change from P 1A was in the power units, where the limited-thrust Sapphires were to be replaced by Rolls Royce Avons (subsequently Avon RA24R Mk 210s) which were described by Mr Page as the largest, lightest and most suitable engines then available. Development of the Avon had increased its diameter, so the installation of a pair, if the staggered layout of the P 1A was to be retained, called for a complete redesign of the fuselage.

The Avon engines developed a dry thrust of 11,250 lb, which increased to 14,350 lb, with after-burning in the Mk1 and 1A. This was not fully modulated but the engines were provided with four after-burner nozzle settings for fixed thrust outputs, thrust in the first setting being varied by changes in engine speed. The power available was almost twice that of the P 1 and, in addition to the changes needed to accommodate the extra diameter, it was also necessary to pay close attention to a revised air intake. The elliptical shape of the P 1 gave way to a circular intake, in the centre of which there was a conical body; this simple two-shock intake, with no complicated bleeds or pressure-relief systems, was evolved to provide a duct giving high-pressure recovery and low drag. It was capable of operating over a wide speed range, being highly efficient at subsonic speeds, and achieved an optimised flow pattern around Mach 2 by deflecting the shock cone outside the intake lip. The cone provided an ideal installation for the Ferranti radar housing, when it formed a pressurised, removable capsule. The thrust reserve available was such that although there was choke in the transonic phase, the phenomenon lasted only a few moments and had no side effects. One situation that did occur as a result of this intake system, which is often mentioned in many of the papers covering Lightning flights, was the phenomenon of intake buzz, this being created by oscillations caused by the airflow and intake geometry not being matched at various Mach numbers.

The choice of design parameters avoided this peculiar situation, which could have had serious fatigue effects on the engine and intake duct. Aerodynamic notes comparing the performance of the P 1B, *XA847*, with the prototype P 1A, *WG760*, specifically refer to the likelihood of buzz occurring at high Mach numbers, but it was felt that this would not happen below Mach 1.8, which at that time, was beyond the limits set for the particular aircraft concerned. If it did occur, the remedy was to lose speed without reducing rpm, for example by shutting down the reheat and climbing. In the event, intake buzz was not experienced until Mach 2 was reached and it never caused serious problems. However, it is interesting to note that one F 3, *XP701*, which served with Nos 29 and 111 Squadrons, was continually being reported by its pilots as giving all the symptoms of intake buzz throughout a wide range of Mach numbers. Investigation eventually traced this to loose ballast weights in the nose-wheel bay and not the aerodynamic phenomena. Apart from the intake changes, the fuselage was also modified in many other areas. The pilot's position was raised, thus introducing a new canopy that had to be faired into a dorsal spine, which was used to house operational equipment including the iso-propyl-nitrate tanks for the Plessey starter, voltage regulators and HF igniters. Nose-wheel retraction was changed so that the wheel moved straight forward into a compartment formed by the lower, centre-body, mounting strut. This meant that it had to be non-steerable, but on the

Above *The first of three P 1Bs, XA847, was the first British aircraft to fly at Mach 2.00 on November 25 1958. The lines of the F 1 Lightning are now clearly beginning to evolve. This aircraft is on display in the RAF Museum Hendon with a modified fin (BAe).*

credit side, it no longer had to swivel to lie flat in its housing. The shape of the air brakes was modified and they were moved ahead of the fin to avoid trim changes which had been evident on the P 1. As previously mentioned, the flaps were also changed and later became containers for additional fuel to supplement the wing tanks.

Before the first flight of the P 1B, the potential of the aircraft had been recognised and an order for 50 aircraft was placed. The first 20 of these, *(XG307–XG313* and *XG325–XG337)* were to be pre-production aircraft used for development and familiarisation work; the remaining 30 were to be designated Lightning F 1 and to be production aircraft for the RAF, these being *XM134–XM147* and *XM163–XM168*. The two original P 1As were flown very hard and the second was fitted with twin 30 mm Adens with which it commenced firing tests in 1956; it carried these tests through to their logical conclusion — supersonic firing — in 1957, before going to the RAE where it was used for low-speed stability tests; at the end of its useful life it became an instructional airframe at Henlow, and now resides in the Air and Space Museum, Manchester, which was opened in 1983. The first airframe, *WG760*, was used at Warton for general-handling flying and was dismantled in 1962 to become an instructional airframe at St Athan and then the gate guardian at Henlow in 1967.

Chapter 3

Into production and service

The original conception of the P 1 was to provide the basis from which a supersonic interceptor, designed to reach high altitude in the shortest possible time, intercept the enemy and then destroy him with cannons or missiles, could be evolved. In the mid-1950s though, the classic stern chaser was still seen as the epitome of a fighter and it was realised that airborne 'loiter' time would be severely restricted by the jet engines' voracious appetite for fuel (flight refuelling then being in its infancy), which made the ability to climb quickly essential. In many ways the interception pattern of the period was similar to that used by the Luftwaffe when operating the Me 163 whose rocket motor took it to the bombers' altitude very quickly. The P 1's ability to achieve the climb requirement was in no doubt from the time the first P 1B, with its Avon engines on dry thrust only, went to 30,000 ft and Mach 1.2 on its maiden flight. The unique engine layout and high ratio of thrust to weight made the aircraft superior to anything flying in 1957 and, even today, it is a formidable combination which can match many later designs for point-to-point interceptors. Indeed, it is worth reflecting on what the Lightning might have achieved if its development had not been retarded by a restrictive budget, narrow-minded politicians and a total lack of foresight by those in authority, who convinced themselves that the manned fighter was a thing of the past.

It is somewhat ironic that on the day the first P 1B (*XA847*) made its maiden flight, the Minister of Defence at the time, Duncan Sandys, announced his plans for the future defence of Great Britain in the form of his now infamous 1957 Defence White Paper. Sandys had been appointed by Prime Minister Harold Macmillan in January 1957 who defined Sandys' task in the following statement: 'He will be responsible for formulating a new defence policy which will secure a substantial reduction in expenditure and manpower, and it will also be his job to prepare a plan for reshaping and reorganising the armed forces.' This simple and direct statement sent a chill through the boardrooms of industries connected with defence but, as is often the case, each company thought it would be spared the axe of whatever cuts in expenditure might be envisaged and carried out.

On the morning of April 4 1957, the P 1B was taken into the air for the first time by Wing Commander Beamont who accelerated it to Mach 1.2, carried out preliminary handling tests and landed after an uneventful flight, 25 minutes later. That afternoon Duncan Sandys produced his White Paper which, in simple terms, stated that he saw no future for the manned military aircraft, claiming that all offensive and defensive roles could adequately be met by missiles, which were cheaper and more cost-effective.

Sandys' statement was a severe blow to the armed forces, as well as the defence industry which, less than a year before, had been caused no alarm by the Statement of Defence, contained within the 1956 Air Estimates, that held that, 'For some time to come the manned fighter must continue to provide the backbone of our defence system. The

Above *P 1B* XA847, *now fitted with a ventral tank, banks away from the camera aircraft to show off this addition. Note the open dive brakes forward of the fin* (BAe).

firepower and lethality of fighter aircraft will be markedly increased by equipping them with air-to-air guided missiles. The first generation of missiles will become available in the course of 1956–57. They will be brought into service with a special mark of Swift and will be used to gain experience of this type of weapon. Although manned fighter aircraft and their weapons will improve, the surface-to-air guided missile may well play a predominant part in the air defence. A production order has been placed for these weapons for trials with the air defence system.'

It could be argued that there was a hint of things to come within the last two sentences, but quite clearly the new minister did not share his predecessor's views that there was a long-term future for manned fighters. He also showed incredible naivety in believing those who advised him that a missile system, which in 1956 was only being ordered for test purposes, could be advanced enough a few months later to provide total offensive and defensive capabilities.

Nonetheless, the Defence Estimate in 1958 for the procurement of aircraft, was reduced by £8 million from the 1956 figure of £165 million and many projects, including Avro's supersonic bomber, the Saunders Roe SR 53, the thin-wing Javelin, Fairey FD 2 derivatives and high-speed research aircraft, were all ruthlessly axed. The Lightning was advanced enough to avoid being dropped and it was also seen as being essential for the defence of Great Britain in height bands beyond the reach of the current first-line fighter — the aged Meteor 8 — and its successor, the Hawker Hunter. But there were few within the 'corridors of power' at Whitehall who could see a rosy future for the aircraft, firmly believing that Sandys' missile-defence umbrella would see it phased out after a very short period. This philosophy clearly had a long-term effect on expenditure as far as the Lightning was concerned and, by the time it was realised that the 1957 White Paper was wrong and that there was very much a future for manned aircraft, the vast development potential of the Lightning had been overtaken by foreign aircraft. However, all was not lost for, in the mid-1960s, when Whitehall reversed its policies, the BAC were able to carry out development work on extending its range and armament capabilities which brought orders from Saudia Arabia and Kuwait. Until this time, such work on the aircraft had been frustrated as though the BAC knew its design potential, the RAF showed little interest in this and the Treasury even less in providing the money.

Although there was just cause for jubilation at Warton on that April day in 1957, the rest of the aeronautical industry in the United Kingdom was thrown into a pit of despair. By the time the White Paper was proved to be misguided in its assumptions, it had ensured that Britain was never likely to become a major supplier of aviation equipment to NATO countries.

The provision of three P 1B prototypes and the 20 pre-production airframes, enabled work to proceed across a very wide spectrum thus, in theory, reducing the time of entry into service. In practice, however, although the idea was sound and had been adopted in other countries with considerable success, there was a problem in handling such a large batch of what were virtually prototype aircraft. Warton had to provide back-up facilities for all aircraft at whichever establishment they were operating from and at times there was a real danger of the available fleet being grounded, thus halting progress. As it was, this did not occur although at times it looked to be very much a possibility. The end result was that the Lightning did enter service earlier than it would have if every aspect of its flight testing, weapons' systems, radar equipment and ancillary components had relied on just three airframes, but the time saved was not as great as that originally estimated.

In April 1957 Flight Test Programme AF/P1/50 was issued for *XA847* (incidentally referred to in all official company papers as the Third Prototype) and this shows that a total of 72 flights in four phases was being aimed for. The phases and their aims were:

Phase 1
21 Flights. Initial flying consisting primarily of a pilot assessment of the handling qualities of the airframe and engine within a defined flight limitation. The limitation was defined as 500 kts below 25,000 ft, 550 kts above that, 5g normal acceleration in a clean condition and 4g with ventral tank fitted. Once cleared within these limits the aircraft could be gradually taken to Mach 1.7, which was in fact the clearance figure required before entry into RAF service.

Phase 2
12 Flights. Airspeed System Development. This involved the aircraft in calibration of all three pitot static systems at high and low altitude. At high altitude, this was to be done in conjunction with an A & AEE Venom and, at low altitude by runs past Blackpool Tower, at speeds from 130 kts with flaps and undercarriage down to 300 kts in a clean condition.

Phase 3
34 Flights. Complete Speed Clearance of the Clean Aircraft. This was broken down into subsections covering flutter, lateral stability at high Mach numbers, stick force and buffet, and an assessment of performance through the speed range of Mach 0.8–1.7 at 36,000, 40,000 and 50,000 ft.

Phase 4
5 or 15 Flights. Blue Jay and Ventral Tank Limits. These flights were to investigate the aerodynamic limits imposed by the carriage of missiles and the fitting of a ventral tank,

the most important being the effect on lateral stability at high Mach numbers. The difference in the quantity of proposed flights was to cover any problems encountered with the aircraft in a Blue-Jay and ventral-tank configuration.

Within six weeks of the aircraft's first flight the Mach 1.7 requirement had been accomplished and it became apparent that the aircraft still had plenty of energy in hand, since tests indicated that the classical situation of total thrust equalling drag, would not occur until at least Mach 2.2.

On November 25 1958, Beamont took *XA847* to Mach 2.0 and reported that there were no difficulties, the aircraft responding beautifully in all phases of the flight. The P 1B therefore became the first British aircraft to fly at twice the speed of sound and this was duly commemorated by a plate on the port side of the aircraft. By this time the fourth aircraft, *XA853*, had joined the programme, having made its maiden flight in the hands of Dizzy de Villiers, a BAC test pilot, on September 5 1957. The fifth aircraft, which was in fact the third P 1B, was *XA856*; its maiden flight, with Beamont at the controls, took place on January 3 1958 and it was used by Rolls Royce for development of the Avon, being delivered to Hucknall on its 35th flight by Rolls Royce test pilot, J. Heyworth.

A month before the Mach 2.0 flight, the aircraft had been given the name 'Lightning' at a simple ceremony at the RAE, Farnborough, on October 23 1958, when the Chief of the Air Staff, Sir Dermot Boyle, broke a bottle of champagne over the nose of an aircraft which had been suitably polished for the occasion. An English Electric press release issued at that time, stated that the aircraft, in both single- and two-seat versions was in large-scale production for the RAF, and that the company anticipated that it would continue to be operated for the following ten years. At the time of writing (1983) two squadrons based in the United Kingdom, Nos 5 and 11, still operate the Lightning from RAF Binbrook, so the company statement turned out to be somewhat pessimistic, which is perhaps not too surprising since it came barely a year after the 1957 White Paper.

The three P 1Bs continued to carry out important work although they were now being joined by aircraft from the pre-production batch of 20, most of which were earmarked for special tasks, thus enabling overall development of many aspects of the aircraft to be carried out at a faster pace than would have been possible on just the original five airframes. By the time the three P 1Bs were pensioned off, they had completed a total of 1,060 flights of which *XA847* had contributed the lion's share, with a total of 468. This aircraft was fitted with a dorsal extension to its fin as a first step towards increasing the fin area that was to follow on the F 2 and F 3; *XA847* was also used at Farnborough in trials testing a new method of stopping aircraft with brake failure, by taxying at various speeds into a gravel bed. It was eventually taken to the RAF museum at Hendon where it is still on public view. The second aircraft, *XA853*, flew a total of 153 hrs 25 mins in its 296 flights (in fact only 52 hrs less than *XA847*) during which time its main objective was to test the gun installation. Its last flight took place on May 3 1963, by which time only the front part of the fuselage was original, the rear having been replaced following an in-flight fire. Most of the aircraft was destroyed on the fire dump at Boscombe Down, but the mainplanes were returned to Warton where they continued to be used on destruction tests so, even after finishing its useful flying life, the aircraft continued to play an important part in the development of the Lightning. The fifth airframe, *XA856*, was used extensively by Rolls Royce in connection with development of the Avon and was eventually struck off charge on June 1 1967, having completed 296 flights. The first of the pre-production batch, *XG307*, made its maiden flight on April 3 1958 from Samlesbury where it had been the first Lightning built. This was followed on the 16th of the following month by *XG308*, after which there was a steady flow until all 20 aircraft had been completed and flown by September 1959.

Opposite *An unusual picture, showing test pilot Don Knight ejecting over Warton from XG311 on July 31 1963, when the aircraft's port undercarriage leg failed to lower. The Lightning crashed into the sea (BAe).*

Above *Part of the pre-production batch of P 1Bs in wintry conditions at Warton. XG309 was scrapped in June 1968 and XG310 in 1971. The latter was the first aircraft to be fitted with the increased-area, pointed fin and was also the first machine to have the square-topped F 3 fin (BAe).*

These development aircraft formed a vital part of Lightning development for, in this aircraft, British industry was embarking not on just the production of a revolutionary interceptor, but a total weapons system comprising, advanced radar and electronics, sophisticated control systems, powerful engines and a highly developed airframe. Each of the 20 pre-production aircraft were assigned specific tasks and though clearly it would be impossible to go into all these in detail, to illustrate the work being carried out it is worth quoting part of the programme laid down for June 1957 covering the flight-test clearance of aircraft with Blue Jay (later to be Firestreak) missiles.

Aircraft nominated for this phase of development were, two of the three P 1Bs, *XA847* and *XA853*, and four of the pre-production batch, *XG308, XG309, XG311* and *XG327*. These six aircraft were to be used for handling trials, flame-out and dispersion firings, jettison, vibration, acquisition and aircraft services, as well as engineering and operational sortie studies. Handling trials were to be carried out mainly by *XA847* and *XG308* before each series of air-firing trials, and the aircraft were to carry two handling missiles to establish carriage limits within the flight envelope. Air firing was to be done at the government-owned RAE Aberporth Range, or the RAF range at Boulmer if Aberporth proved unsatisfactory. An interesting aside, which came to light later, was that every time a government range was used, a charge was made to the company. Whilst it must be appreciated that certain facilities and staff had to be provided, it does tend to highlight a typically 'British' situation, whereby a company trying to develop an aircraft or weapons' system, with export potential that could benefit the whole country's economy, could be financially penalised by having to make high payments to the very administration it was helping.

Of course, the Lightning was not the only aircraft to be afflicted but these test-range charges are indicative of the muddled thinking and attitude of government officials, who would burden almost any project with unnecessary costs. It has been estimated that using the range once a week for a six month period cost the BAC over £25,000, at a time when they were confident that the Lightning had a vast potential in export fields. However, such bureaucratic and political incompetence is not unique and is really beyond the scope of this book, other than to illustrate that a fine aircraft suffered from it.

To return to the test programme, the flights arranged for *XG309* will be sufficient to show just a small part of what was involved in this particular development; AF/P1/51, page 8, details this as follows:

1 Programme
1.1 Jettison trials.
      1.1.1   Ground jettison — two rounds.
      1.1.2   Airborne jettison, 150–250 kts, 5,000 ft — Four rounds.
1.2 Flame-out and fixed-fin dispersion firings.
      1.2.1   1.3 M, 50,000 ft — 4 rounds.
      1.2.2   1.3 M, 600–650 kts — 4 rounds.
      1.2.3   0.9 M, 5,000 ft — 2 rounds.
1.3 Airframe distortion and vibration — 2 rounds.
1.4 Target Acquisition Trials.   }
1.5 Preliminary supplies-system and engineering trials. } 2 rounds

2   Trials venue
The aircraft will be based at Warton throughout the trials. The air jettison trials will be conducted at any suitable range. Air firings will be carried out at the Aberporth G.W. range, or RAF Boulmer range. On air firing sorties detailed 1.2.1 and 1.2.2 above, the aircraft will land at RNAS Brawdy for refuelling, before and after each firing.

3   Duration
Trials are scheduled to commence in February 1958 and should be completed by the end of July 1958.

4   Missiles
4.1 Jettison ground and airborne 6 type 1B
4.2 Flame out and dispersion, 10 type 5 (with telemetry).
4.3 Distortion and Vibration, 2 type 2
4.4 Acquisition and aircraft services, 2 type 3

5   Instrumentation
As detailed on pages 11–13, selected to suit the particular weapon role.

The above report is quoted verbatim and the reference to other pages cover the technicalities of the system being tested at the time. It is interesting to note that the programme suffered some slippage since *XG309* did not make its maiden flight until June 23 1958, some four months after it was scheduled to have become involved in these particular weapon trials.

The 20 pre-production aircraft differed little from the P 1B except that after the first three aircraft had been built the fin and rudder area was increased by about 30 per cent to compensate for the destabilising effect of the externally carried Firestreak missiles. *XG310* was the first aircraft to fly with the new taller fin on July 17 1958 and it was subsequently also the first aircraft to be fitted with the square-top F 3 fin, with which it appeared at Farnborough in 1963 for that year's SBAC show. All 20 development-batch aircraft were built with or modified to have the new taller fin, apart from *XG311*, which retained the smaller fin throughout its life; a life that included a period of tropical trials in Aden in 1961 and ended on July 31 1963 on its 238th flight when it crashed into the sea near Warton.

Development of the Airpass radar system progressed, with its installation in trials' aircraft such as the Canberra, the Meteor and the evergreen Dakota, as well as in Lightning *XG312*, which spent most of its flying life with Ferranti at Bitteswell on radar development. This aircraft was finally grounded in 1966 after giving its pilot, J. Cockburn, something of a shock when the windscreen shattered at Mach 0.9 at 37,000 ft; it was landed successfully but never flew again, eventually being scrapped in April 1972 with 303 hrs 53 minutes to its credit. Mid-way through the development batch, additional fuel tank capacity was introduced, which helped to overcome the problem of limited duration that had been evident during the early flight trials. Apart from *XG332*, which was used throughout its life by the BAC and de Havilland for Firestreak and Red Top trials, all the pre-production batch aircraft were at sometime or another used by the A & AEE, the RAE and English Electric on a flying programme that was intensive and aimed to prove the aircraft suitable for service requirements within the shortest possible time.

The first production order for the Lightning was placed in November 1956. The first 20 aircraft ordered were the pre-production batch and while these were carrying out their vital tasks, work on the remaining 20 continued. On October 29 1959, *XM134*, which was the first true production Lightning, made its maiden flight from Samlesbury to Warton, once again the pilot being 'Bee' Beamont. This flight was not without incident as the aircraft lost part of its starboard undercarriage-leg fairing, but suffered no other damage. The production batch of F 1 Lightnings, as the aircraft was now designated, was for twenty aircraft in the serial ranges *XM134–XM147* and *XM163–XM168*; these all flowed steadily off the production line until the last aircraft, *XM167* made its maiden flight on July 14 1960, by which time the RAF had started to take delivery; incidentally, the last airframe, *XM168*, was retained at Warton for structural tests and never flew.

The F 1 was armed with two 30 mm Aden cannons, mounted high on the nose either side of the cockpit, and two de Havilland Firestreak heat-seeking missiles on pylons either side of the nose, just forward of the wing leading edge. A removable pack under the fuselage could carry either 48 2-in rockets, or two more Aden cannons; these weapon packs could be interchanged in less than an hour and a Lightning in any armament configuration could be refuelled and re-armed in less than ten minutes.

A number of service pilots had flown the P 1B during its flying programme; one of them, Sqn Ldr Jimmy Dell, who was permanently seconded to the company's flight-operations department, became the second pilot to record 1,000 Lightning flights, Beamont of course being the first. The aircraft was also flown by pilots from the United States who took glowing reports back to America, especially about the aircraft's climb rate and it was hoped that such reports might prompt the Americans into looking into the Lightning a little closer with a view to ordering it, though sadly this came to nothing. If they had, it would have given English Electric the unique distinction of being the only British aircraft manufacturer to supply the Americans with two combat aircraft, the other being the Canberra which the USAF used successfully for many years.

The final three development-batch aircraft, although not built totally to the final specification, were considered to be sufficiently close to it to be passed to the Central Fighter Establishment (CFE) for service handling trials. The three aircraft were *XG334*, *XG335* and *XG336*, coded A, B, and C, the first of which was delivered to Coltishall on December 23 1959 by Sqn Ldr J. Nicholls, who must have been regarded as something of a true Santa Claus with a genuine Mach 2 fighter for RAF Fighter Command (as it was then still called). At Coltishall, the three Lightnings were used by the Air Fighting Development Squadron (AFDS) for operational evaluation; the experience gained by the unit's highly qualified pilots was compiled into useful information for operational squadrons when they started to be re-equipped with the aircraft.

Unfortunately only three months after taking delivery of the aircraft, the AFDS lost *XG334* 'A', when Sqn Ldr Harding could not lower the undercarriage and was forced to eject, the aircraft falling into the sea just off Wells-next-the-Sea. This occurred on March 5 1960 at which time *XG334* had completed only 34 flights and accumulated 23 hrs 35 mins flying time. Two months later, the first of four F 1 Lightnings, *XM135* 'D', was delivered to the AFDS by D.M. Knight, on May 25, followed by *XM136* 'E', *XM137* 'F' and *XM138* 'G', all of which arrived during June 1960. By this time No 74 Squadron also based at Coltishall, had been named as the first operational squadron to receive the Lightning, and their first machine, *XM165* coded 'A', which had first flown on May 30 1960, was delivered on June 29 by Jimmy Dell, thus becoming the first Lightning to enter RAF squadron service.

Before looking at the Lightning in squadron service, it would be wise to detail how development continued and to include that of the two-seat trainer versions, so that continuity of service covering the different marks and versions can be maintained.

Below *A F 1 of No 74 Squadron on reheat tests at Warton. This aircraft was later used by 226 OCU and the Leuchars TFF, before going into store at 60 MU in 1972* (BAe).

Chapter 4

Lightning lineage

The ability of the Lightning to climb to 30,000 ft in two and a half minutes from the time the pilot released the brakes was a feat that no fighter in service in the mid-1950s could emulate. In fact some 30 years later, there are still very few aircraft that can, but it must be remembered that the strategy of aerial combat has changed a great deal during the same period. The whole essence of interception, in 1957, was the ability to get a fighter to the height of an incoming bomber as quickly as possible and any method of shortening the point-to-point interception time was well worth considering.

English Electric therefore took a great deal of interest in the Double Scorpion rocket motor then being developed by a company within their own group, D. Napier & Son Ltd. The installation of a rocket motor in the Lightning would not only boost its climb rate but also increase its service ceiling as at very high altitude, where the rarefied air made the jet engine very inefficient, the rocket motor came into its element. Steps were therefore taken to design a packet containing not only the Scorpion rocket but its high-test peroxide oxidant (a type of fuel additive to give increased power), which used kerosene drawn from the aircraft's normal fuel tanks. The pack was jettisonable and could be refuelled *in situ* on the aircraft. The rocket motor was extremely small, being just under a metre in length and 60 cm wide, but its two tubes, which could be fired independently, developed thrust well beyond what could be envisaged from such a small engine. The Double Scorpion was installed in a Canberra B2 *(WK163)* test bed which in August 1957 went to 70,310 ft, well beyond the contemporary world altitude record. A similar aircraft was lost the following April when it encountered difficulties after firing the twin Scorpion at high-altitude; the crew, Flt Lt P. de Salis and Flying Officer P. Lowe, ejected safely at about 56,000 ft, which at that time was the highest ejection on record. It was intended to fit the installation to a P 1B but the requirement was cancelled and the Lightning never had the opportunity of showing its prowess with this form of power unit.

A logical improvement in the early days of development was to increase the aircraft's range, which even with the 250-gallon ventral tank, was hardly enough to allow a high-speed climb, acceleration to interception speed and one pass at a target. The obvious answer was in-flight refuelling, followed by a long-range version with increased tank capacity. The 1957 White Paper had made money a short commodity, especially for the development of systems on a fighter that it was believed would soon be replaced by missiles, so it is perhaps not surprising therefore that the RAF could only muster lukewarm enthusiasm for spending money on what would possibly be a very short-term investment.

The prototype P 1B, *XA847*, was fitted with a dry-link flight-refuelling probe and after successful installation and flight trials, it was introduced onto *XM169*, which was the first of the second batch of 30 airframes covered by the initial order of 50 F 1s. This aircraft became the first F 1A, of which 30 were scheduled for production but only 28 built,

XM217 and *XM218* being the serials allocated to the two not produced.

The first F 1A made its maiden flight from Samlesbury on August 16 1960 and, in addition to the refuelling probe beneath the port wing, it was fitted with UHF radio. Changes to internal equipment and a rerun of the electrical cables, brought the only difference between the F 1 and F 1a, namely an external duct along the lower fuselage. The second F 1A to fly, *XM170*, which took to the air in the hands of J. Isherwood on September 12 1960, had possibly the shortest life of any Lightning, this being the 14 minutes of its maiden flight. During a pre-flight test at Warton the aircraft's electrical systems became contaminated by mercury following a battery leak and the machine was written off. It was subsequently mounted on a 'Queen Mary' lorry and used in the Lord Mayor's Show in London in 1961, before becoming instructional airframe *7877M* at RAF Newton. The original F 1A was retained at Warton where it was used mainly on flight-refuelling trials, making 223 flights before going to 111 Squadron on October 14 1964. The first F 1A to join an RAF squadron was *XM172*, which made its maiden flight on October 10 1960 and was delivered to No 56 Squadron at Wattisham by P. Hillwood on December 14 1960, its first squadron identity letter being 'B'.

The next single-seat Lightning was the F 2, for which an order of 44 was placed, these being in the serial ranges *XN723–XN735* and *XN767–XN797*. The first of these aircraft, *XN723*, was flown on July 11 1961 by J. Dell and was used for F 2 appraisal at Boscombe Down; it crashed on March 25 1964 at Hucknall while in the hands of Rolls Royce, its pilot on that occasion being D. Withnal, who used the Martin Baker Mk 4BS ejection seat to save his life when the number 2 engine caught fire. The F 2 was externally similar to the F 1A, retaining the pointed fin/rudder and extended cable-ducting along the fuselage side, with the only recognisable difference being the intake duct on the spine for the aircraft's DC stand-by generator. Internally, the F 2 was fitted with partial OR 946 flight instrumentation (without the strip speed display), offset TACAN and a liquid-oxygen breathing system. The Avon 210s exhausted through revised tailpipes and introduced, for the first time, a fully variable, reheat system in place of the four-position reheat used on the F 1 and F 1A.

Top left *This F 1A first flew on September 20 1960. It served with No 56 Squadron and collided with XM179 on June 6 1963, after which it landed safely, although the other aircraft was destroyed* (English Electric).

Left and below left *The Scorpion Canberra WK163 showing the installation of the rocket motor, which was designed as a fitment for the Lightning* (M.P. Marsh).

Below *A line-up of F 1As of the Binbrook TFF taken in December 1972. The short cable ducting can be clearly seen and is worth comparing with photographs of other versions. Note the faired-in gun ports* (RAF Binbrook).

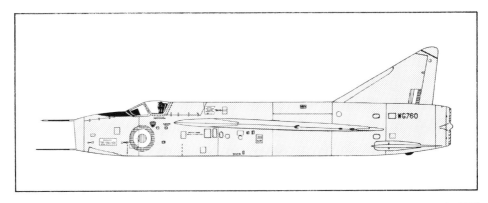

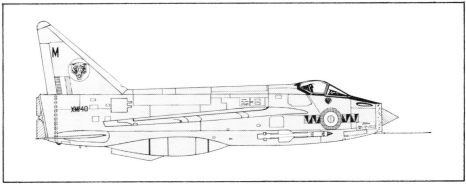

Top *P 1A* WG760, *the first prototype, in overall natural metal finish with matt black anti-glare panel.*

Above *Lightning F 1* XM140 *'M', No 74(F) Squadron, RAF Coltishall, 1962. Machine in overall silver finish (a mixture of aluminium painted surfaces and natural metals of various surface finishes) and with polished metal intake ring and pitot tube; matt black anti-glare panel and cockpit framing.*

Below *An Aden cannon-armed F 2, without its ventral tank. This aircraft was destroyed in a crash on March 25 1964, when on loan to Rolls-Royce* (BAe).

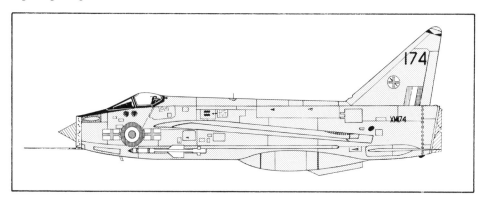

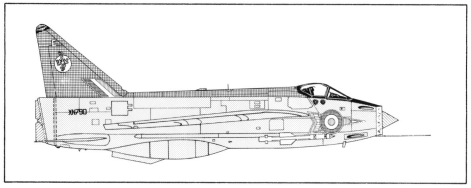

Top *Lightning F 1A* XM174, *No 226 OCU, RAF Coltishall, 1966. Finish as for F 1.*

Above *Lightning F 2* XN790 'E', *No 92(F) Squadron, RAF Leconfield, 1964. Finish as F 1, with gloss dark blue dorsal spine and fin surfaces (note four guns in nose of this version).*

Below *Roland Beamont with* XN725 *before a test flight* (BAe).

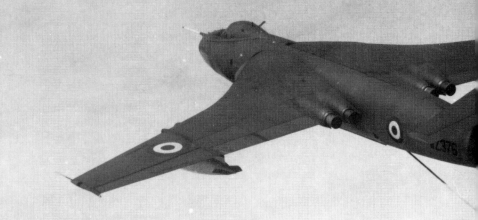

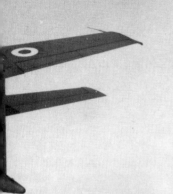

Background photograph *The first F 1A, XM169, was fitted with a production-type refuelling probe and used extensively in tests. It is seen here with a Valiant tanker (BAe).*

Inset *Many pilots claim the F 2A to be the most successful Lightning. This view of a 19 Squadron aircraft clearly shows the large ventral tank and cambered leading edge, as well as the arrestor hook housed in the rear of the tank (RAF Germany).*

Above XN725 *was built as an F 2 and converted to the F 3 prototype; it later became the first F 3 to be fitted with the cambered wing. The over-wing tanks are dummies* (BAe).

Below *The F 3 prototype pulls away from the photographic aircraft* (BAe).

Bottom *The F 3 prototype shows off the dummy wing-tank installation. The finlets on top of the tanks were later discarded* (BAe).

Leaving aside for a moment the two-seat version to be dealt with separately, the next single-seat Lightning was the F 3, which was the first of the second generation or, as English Electric referred to it in a 1963 press release, the 'stretched' version. This rather oblique reference was not to any major changes in the dimensions of the aircraft, but merely a reference to the ability to adapt the basic airframe to accommodate more modern weapons and avionics. The F 3 used Avon series 300 engines with a thrust of 13,500 lb each, boosted to 16,000 by reheat, more than twice the power available to the original P 1A. Another important change was to the weapons' system, which now used the de Havilland Red Top missile and an improved Ferranti Airpass airborne-interception radar known as AI 23B. The aircraft was not fitted with any Aden cannons and was therefore purely a missile-armed interceptor. This was perhaps a rather odd decision, as, from the very early days of air-to-air combat, the pilot has always been master of his own destiny, his survival depending not only on his skill in operating the aircraft, but also his ability in air gunnery. The use of two missiles, locked onto their target by a computer and fired when the aircraft was in the position to achieve the best results, with the pilot acting basically as a monitor, did not seem to evoke the normal picture conjured in the mind of a fighter pilot. This is perhaps typified by a former commanding officer of No 23 Squadron Capt L.A. Strange, who wrote in his memoirs of the First World War, '. . . every man who goes into the air in a fighting machine is a gun layer—first and last. . .', a statement that has more than an element of truth and one which stands the test of time. After all,

Below *An F 3 of No 111 Squadron flying off Malta. The badge above the unit marking on the nose is the Second World War emblem of the Richthofen Geschwader; there is also a Squadron badge above the missile. XP762 made its maiden flight on September 3 1964 and became 'C' with No 111 Squadron on January 26 1965 (Joint Services PR Office).*

Above *One of the batch of 20 pre-production P 1Bs, XG329 was used mainly on the gun-firing programme and by de Havilland on missile work between April and December 1966. It was later fitted with a square fin* (BAe).

cannons can be used to put a warning shot across the bows of an intruder, but a missile cannot. The situation was redressed with the F 6, which could be fitted with cannon armament.

The Red Top missile had a longer burning time than the Firestreak, a more powerful motor, was much more manoeuvrable and allowed collision-course attacks, whereas the Firestreak could only be used in pursuit attacks. To compensate for the larger missiles the aircraft's fin was increased by 15 per cent and the square-cut top was introduced. Other structural changes were also introduced and, apart from the new fin, the most noticeable of these was a further extension of the external cable ducts on the sides of the fuselage. The changes allowed a small increase in fuel to be included but as this was negated, as far as additional range was concerned, by the increased capacity and fuel consumption of the more powerful Avons, the aircraft continued to suffer from short duration and pilots still had to keep a constant 'weather eye' on their fuel states. The F 3 was, of course, fitted with full in-flight refuelling equipment which enabled standing patrols and long deployments to be carried out with the aid of tanker aircraft.

One of the early pre-production batch of 20 P 1Bs, *XG310*, was modified to F 3 standard and made its maiden flight with the larger fin on June 16 1962; interestingly, this aircraft was also the first of the batch to have originally flown with the taller, pointed, production fin. It was displayed as an F 3 at the SBAC Display Farnborough in 1963, although strictly speaking, at this time its only resemblance to the mark was the square-cut fin. Six aircraft in the *XG* serial range of pre-production P 1Bs were used for trials connected with the F 3, *XG327* being the first to be completely modified to F 3 aerodynamic standards. Others to be used were, *XG328, 329, 331, 332* and *335*, the last two being mainly used in Red Top trials by de Havilland. The first true prototype F 3 was *XP693* which was later modified to F 3a standard and, as late as 1972, was still in use on MRCA avionic trials. *XP694* was used extensively by Ferranti on AI 23 development programme and made 147 flights on this work before being delivered to 60 MU, whence it eventually found its way to No 29 Squadron. The first F 3 was delivered to the RAF on January 1 1964 when *XP695* was flown from Warton to Binbrook to be taken on strength by CFE. This aircraft was later returned to Warton in July 1967, where it was updated to the full F 3 standard and was still in use with No 11 Squadron in 1982.

The F 3 was ordered in greater quantity than any other version, a total of 70 in the serial ranges *XP693–XP708, XP735–XP765, XR711–XR728* and *XR747–XR751* being built, although a lot of these were subsequently modified to interim standards or, later, to full F 6 specification. The F 3 certainly introduced a much more sophisticated aeroplane to the RAF and by the time, in 1964, that the BAC, which had taken over English Electric, had officially claimed that the aircraft was so advanced in its equipment that it was

Above *A Lightning F 3 of No 29 Squadron during a training deployment to Cyprus in June 1974* (RAF).

Below XG310 *started life as a pre-production batch P 1B. In this photograph it has been modified to F 3 configuration* (BAe).

Above *A 29 Squadron F 3 which is now 8453M and the gate guardian at RAF Boulmer. The stencilling under the windscreen is the name of the pilot and crew chief* (MoD).

Below *Ventral tanks are not often seen off the aircraft, so the opportunity to record this F 3 tank was taken during a visit to Binbrook* (author).

Opposite *An F 3 of No 29 Squadron* (BAe).

virtually a new interceptor/weapons' system, superior to any other in the world, it was already established in squadron use. The only shortcoming of the F 3, was the problem of fuel capacity but, by now, moves were afoot to correct this and produce the definitive version of the aircraft.

Since the 1957 White Paper, it had become very obvious that the Lightning was not to be the RAF's last manned interceptor and, in 1963, the ministry at last recognised that the new fuel system which had been planned by the manufacturers and constantly rejected was an essential requirement. The Warton design staff developed a new ventral tank with a far greater capacity than the 250 Imp gal of the existing design. The tank was fitted with two fins, to maintain directional stability, and was initially attached to *XP697*, which also appeared with a cambered leading-edge extension. The wing extension had been tried on the P 1A in 1957, and the long tank and ventral fin on *XA847* in 1959, although on the modified F 3 the camber was slightly less than had been originally used. The wing had reduced outer-panel sweep and increased leading-edge camber, so that lift was improved at high angles of attack and subsonic drag was reduced. There was virtually no performance penalty but range was increased by 20 per cent as a result of the increased efficiency of the wing. On the new wing, the ailerons became inset and although the span was unchanged the area was increased by approximately 13 sq ft. The overall effect of the wing was not only to improve the aircraft's range but also its high-altitude performance, particularly at subsonic speeds, thus increasing its effective operational ceiling. Handling at low speeds in the circuit was also affected, where the increased wing area helped to maintain lift at lower throttle settings. On the debit side, slightly higher stick forces were required during take-off and landing, and there was a slightly slower response in the rolling plane, but overall the advantages of the cambered wing far outweighed the disadvantages.

The range of the aircraft was also increased by the introduction of overwing ferry tanks each containing 260 Imp gal. Because of the location of the undercarriage it was not possible to mount the long-range tanks in the underwing positions normally used, so pylons were installed above the wings and these later provided locations for alternative weapon pods. The enlarged ventral (which was not jettisonable) and the two wing tanks

increased the Lightning's fuel capacity by over 1,000 gal and this together with the additional range produced by the improved aerodynamics of the wing, gave the aircraft an endurance that could only have been dreamed about by pilots of the earlier versions. Naturally it proved extremely attractive to the service who instituted a change in their requirements for the F 3, with the latter half of the contract being updated to include the latest modifications. The aircraft was initially referred to as the F 3a or F 3ER/6/Int (Interim F 6) but was quickly designated F 6 for RAF service.

The first F 6 was *XP697*, which had originally been the fifth F 3 production aircraft; it made its maiden flight as an F 6 on April 17 1964 in the hands of 'Bee' Beamont. It continued on the development-batch flying programme and was used to test the effect of the weapons' pack, carrying 2-in rocket projectiles, on the aerodynamics of the aircraft. The first production F 3, *XP693*, was also modified to F 3a standard as were two production F 2s, *XN724* and *XN725*. The latter machine was the first to fly with the cambered leading edge and was also fitted with Avon 301s. When it was initially

Left *This F 3, in the markings of 2T Squadron of 226 OCU, was the fourth production aircraft; it was used by CFE Binbrook and at Boscombe Down on Red Top trials, before being modified to full F 3 standard in July 1967 (Peter March).*

Below *The Lightning always was a thirsty aeroplane! Here two F 6s of No 11 Squadron replenish their tanks from a Victor K 2 of 232 OCU (MoD).*

converted to F 3 standard, it also flew with a variety of ventral tanks. It spent its whole life on experimental flying, including simulated Concorde 'noise' tests in 1972. The first production F 6 was one of a batch of 16 (*XR752–XR767*) which were really interim models; although externally identical to the F 6, they lacked the necessary strong points for the overwing tanks and some internal modifications.

XR752 made its maiden flight from Samlesbury on June 16 1965 in the hands of 'Dizzy' de Villiers and was delivered to CFE at Binbrook on November 26 the same year by Sqn Ldr Sawyer, just ten days after *XR753* had been taken on strength by the same unit to become the RAF's first F 6. Subsequently 15 of the 16 interim airframes were withdrawn from service, as full-standard F 6s became available, and were modified to the full standard before being returned to service. The one exception was *XR766* which crashed into the sea, east of Montrose, on a sortie from Leuchars on September 7 1967, with the pilot, Sqn Ldr R. Blackburn, ejecting safely. The first full-standard F 6 was *XR768* which was delivered to No 74 Squadron on August 1 1966. The production quantity of full-standard F 6s was 39, these being in the serial batches, *XR768–XR773*, *XS893–XS904* and *XS918–XS938*.

Right *A production F 6 with the definitive over-wing tanks. This aircraft was used by Nos 11 and 56 Squadrons and was with No 5 Squadron, coded 'AD', at Binbrook in 1983 (BAC).*

Below right *One solution to the fuel problem was the introduction of over-wing tanks for the F 6. This 74 Squadron aircraft shows the port one to advantage, as well as the refuelling probe and its Red Top missiles (MoD).*

Below *The cambered-wing leading edge, refuelling probe and Firestreak missiles of F 6 XR760 are shown to advantage as this No 5 Squadron aircraft turns away. Note the different colours of the missiles (MoD).*

Above *The cable ducting and part of the ventral tank of F 6, XR754 of No 11 Squadron* (R.L. Ward).

Below *A pristine F 6 with all the options* (author's collection).

The appearance at Farnborough in 1962 of a Lightning with the new ventral tank, as well as optional weapon packs which could be fitted into the tank's front, led to conjecture as to its potential in the ground attack role. This was something that the RAF was not too interested in at that time and although, in some publications, it has been suggested that some squadrons did train for this role, there is no supporting evidence. But the increased weaponry available to the Lightning, as a result of the additional strong points, was something that was to be exploited by its manufacturers later on in the export versions.

Some people's thoughts also turned in other directions with regard to increasing the flexibility of the Lightning. The BAC had pioneered variable-sweep wings and, in 1960, Sir George Edwards, then Chairman of Vickers Armstrong, had commented that the Lightning could be an ideal 'swing-wing' test vehicle. Although nothing ever came of this, a design study for a 'navalised' Lightning was in fact undertaken. Basically this aircraft was a T 5 with the large ventral tank (similar to the Saudi T 55); the front portion of the tank carried weapons and the rear arrester gear. The undercarriage was redesigned to retract inwards, the large square-topped fin had a folding section to facilitate storage on board aircraft carriers and the fin also had a much larger dorsal fairing than that associated with the T 5. The outboard sections of the wings were pivoted at about mid-span to allow them to be swept forward, and in this position the span increased from the fully swept 37 ft 7 in to 48 ft 2 in. Overall length of the navalised Lightning, which is referred to on general-arrangement drawings as the Mk 5, was to be 50 ft and the height over the fin stayed at 19 ft 7 in reduced to 16 ft 6 in in the folded position. Missile armament was as for the F 3, as were the associated avionics, though the engines originally envisaged were RB199s. This interesting project never advanced beyond the general-arrangement drawing stage, which is perhaps a great pity since it could have added a very potent weapon to the Royal Navy's inventory.

The final single-seat version of the Lightning to enter RAF service was the F 2a, which was basically the F 2 brought up to F 6 standards. The conversion consisted of adding the enlarged ventral tank and cambered wing, although this was not stressed for over-wing tanks, together with the increased-area fin and arrester gear. The original twin 30 mm Aden cannon installation in the upper nose remained, but with the revised gun pack in the forward part of the ventral tank, the aircraft could be fitted with additional cannons. At the 1970 Farnborough air show, *XN733* appeared fully modified to F 2a standard with

Below *Lightning F 2A, XN781, of No 19 Squadron, RAF Germany, in February 1974. It is fitted with Firestreak missiles and a pair of 30 mm Aden cannons in the upper fuselage* (RAF Gütersloh).

four-cannon armament. Of the original 44 F 2s produced, 32 were converted to F 2a standard, the first of which was *XN795*. *XN795* had originally flown as an F 2 on May 30 1963 and was partially converted on July 9 1964, being fitted only with the revised fin and larger ventral tank. This aircraft retained the straight-leading-edge wing of the original F 2 and was still with the BAC in 1982 on contract work for the MoD, having spent most of its life on development flying, which included 27 mm Mauser gun trials in connection with the MRCA. Of the twelve F 2s not converted, five were purchased by the BAC for use on the Saudi contract, these being *XN729, XN767, XN770, XN796* and *XN797*; two airframes, *XN725* and *XN734*, were used as trials aircraft for the F 3; *XN723* and *XN785* crashed in service; and the residue, *XN768, XN769* and *XN794*, were left as F 2s and served as target facility aircraft with both 19 and 92 Squadrons.

Armament for the RAF Lightnings has been twin missiles and cannons since they were introduced into service. Over the years many proposals were put forward to change the aircraft's armament but for a variety of reasons these were rejected by the service. The addition of pylons in overwing and underwing positions enabled the full potential of the aircraft to be totally investigated and although the RAF, through the CFE at Binbrook, did make certain suggestions and comments relating to additional armament, these were never taken up to the extent that they might have been. The extent to which BAC had investigated a multi-mission Lightning came to light when the private venture F 53 was revealed. This was aimed at the export market and brought deserved orders to the company from two countries in the Middle East.

Wind-tunnel tests in 1966 enabled the optimum positions and geometry of the pylons to be determined; simulator studies were also used to assess flutter characteristics with external stores and to determine the effect of weapon release on the stability of the whole system. Flight trials indicated that although the pylons were positioned to give optimum delivery at subsonic speeds, they were entirely satisfactory throughout the whole speed range, both with and without stores attached. It was feared that buffeting might affect the aircraft's flaps and tailplane when 1,000-lb bombs were carried, but this was found not to be the case.

The BAC also looked for undesirable inertia-coupling effects on manoeuvrability when carrying outboard loads, but again they did not find any. Rolling inertia was of course

Below *F 2A, XN781, of No 19 Squadron flying over the Moehne Dam in February 1974* (RAF Gütersloh).

Above *The formidable range of weaponry available for the F 53 is shown here on* G-AWON *at the 1968 SBAC display. This aircraft became 53-686 and was delivered to Saudi Arabia on April 17 1969* (author).

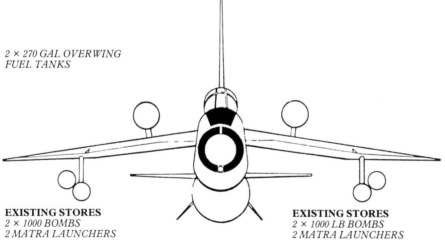

2 × 270 GAL OVERWING FUEL TANKS

EXISTING STORES
2 × 1000 BOMBS
2 MATRA LAUNCHERS

NEW STORES
2 × 540 LB BALLISTIC BOMBS
2 × 540 LB RETARDED BOMBS
2 × 1000 LB RETARDED BOMBS
2 × 50 GAL FIREBOMBS
1 × 100 GAL FIREBOMB
2 BL755 CLUSTER BOMBS
1 CBLS 100 CARRIER

EXISTING STORES
44 × 2 INCH ROCKETS
OR
RECCE PACK
PLUS
2 ADEN GUN PACK
OR
ENGINE HATCH
FUEL TANK

EXISTING STORES
2 × 1000 LB BOMBS
2 MATRA LAUNCHERS

NEW STORES
2 × 540 LB BALLISTIC BOMBS
2 × 540 LB RETARDED BOMBS
2 × 1000 LB RETARDED BOMBS
2 × 50 GAL FIREBOMBS
1 × 100 GAL FIREBOMB
2 BL755 CLUSTER BOMBS
1 CBLS 100 CARRIER

EXTERNAL STORES

Above *The extent of stencilling, as well as the nick-name 'Boss Kat' applied to F 2A XN781 of No 19 Squadron, shows up well on the dark green top surfaces of the Wing Commander's aircraft* (RAF Germany).

increased, but the ailerons were able to cope with this and retain their usual effectiveness. Drastic trim changes with asymmetrical loads were also expected but did not materialise, as aero-elastic effects arising from the bomb carriage influenced the rolling behaviour of the aircraft so as to offset the bomb's inertia. Having cleared all aspects of bomb carriage, the BAC had no problems with the Matra SNEB rocket launchers, which were about the same size as the bombs, but less in weight. Information relating to the weapons' and fuel capacity as external stores is well illustrated by the accompanying drawing.

One of the issues stressed in the 1957 White Paper was the importance of defending the nuclear deterrent, be it by an all-missile or a manned force. Since the Lightning would play a vital role in this, it was necessary to take careful stock of its proposed weapons. As a first-line interceptor it was the aim — albeit an impossible one — that the aircraft be capable of achieving a 100 per cent success rate in the destruction of hostile aircraft intruding into friendly airspace intent on destroying the deterrent. Cannons and conventionally armed air-to-air missiles could not produce the success rate considered desirable and attention was therefore turned to a more effective weapon. Such a weapon was the American-designed 'Genie' missile which was fitted to some American fighters including the F-106. The 'Genie' was fitted with a nuclear warhead and would therefore prove quite lethal if used in the interception of a possibly large formation of hostile bomber aircraft.

In the late 1950s, agreement was reached for the supply of this missile by the United States Government and planning was begun to modify the Lightning to accept it. Changing circumstances, including the revision of thoughts first mooted in the White Paper, contributed to the project being terminated during the early 1960s. Had it gone ahead, 'Genie' would have been mounted in pairs beneath the fuselage, forward of the ventral tank. Full details of the installation are not yet available for publication.

Chapter 5

Two-seat Lightnings

Pilot training during World War 2 followed a pattern of general progression from aircraft like the Tiger Moth or Magister, used for primary *ab initio* flying, through the Harvard or Master, for advanced flying, and then on to twins for bomber pilots, or combat-expired fighters for those destined for single-seaters. The transition from Harvard to Spitfire was a big step, not to be undertaken lightly, or before the Harvard instructor had absolute faith in his pupil. The advent of the jet fighter brought a need for a change in such methods of advancement and although, in the immediate post-war years, the path of the budding fighter pilot was basically similar, the time was not far off when he was able to get the feel of a jet fighter from the pupil's seat in a Meteor 7. This was basically a Meteor IV, with the fuselage stretched to accommodate another seat. The Vampire followed suit, but this time a side-by-side arrangement was favoured. In America, similar paths of progress were followed with the adaptation of the P 80 Shooting Star into the T 33 — some of which are still in service — and, much later, side-by-side aircraft like the Cessna T-37.

The advent of the Swift and Hunter did not bring an immediate requirement for a comparable-performance trainer, it being considered that the Vampire and Meteor provided a satisfactory stepping stone. The Swift was a disaster in its designed role, but the Hunter went from success to success and it is perhaps a little surprising that a two-seat version was not envisaged in the early stages of development. Such was not the case with the Lightning, plans for a dual-controlled version being made as early as 1957 when it was appreciated that the RAF would need such an aircraft for operational training, not only in the basic handling of the Lightning, but also with its weapons' systems.

Originally known as the English Electric P 11, the first dual-controlled version was based on the F 1A. From the start it was always intended that the side-by-side layout should be used, this being preferred in cases where the aircraft was to be more than just a dual-controlled trainer, which in this case was very much so as the two-seat Lightning was to have a full operational capability. Overall dimensions of the basic F 1A were not changed but, from frame 25 to frame 1, that is, moving forward along the aircraft's fuselage in the general-arrangement drawings, the forward fuselage was altered in cross-section shape and width. To accommodate an additional Martin Baker 4BST ejection seat the fuselage was widened by 30 cm (11.5 in), the extra bulk of the seat being no detriment to performance for two reasons; one, the two Aden cannons were removed, thus saving weight and, two, the new fuselage shape coincidentally conformed to 'Area rule' criteria, even though the theory was still in its infancy. Constructed on production jigs, the aircraft was more in the nature of a pre-production machine than a prototype, as it carried the pilot attack-sights and radar scopes and full dual control. Armed with twin Firestreaks, the two-seat Lightning could be a fully operational aircraft in its own right and in such a case the pilot would be freed from the need to supervise the weapons' control systems, as this duty would become the responsibility of the second crew member.

The first example, still known as the P 11, made its maiden flight from Warton on May 6 1959, two weeks' ahead of schedule. Piloted by Roland Beamont, the aircraft was airborne for 30 minutes during which time it exceeded Mach 1 by a comfortable margin. For its maiden flight the two-seat Lightning was finished in natural aluminium but had the correct, for the period, yellow trainer band around wings and fuselage. The aircraft was flown at the 1959 SBAC Display at Farnborough where it appeared carrying Firestreaks and the name 'Lightning T 4' in script below the cockpit. This was the first time that the T 4 designation was officially acknowledged, although some weeks before the French publication, *Aviation Magazine* had referred to it by this number.

On October 1 1959 *XL628* was being flown by Johnny Squier on handling tests at high Mach numbers along a route that took him over the Irish Sea, between the Isle of Man and the mainland. The aircraft was flying at high altitude in excees of Mach 1, when immediately after coming out of a roll the fin collapsed. The Lightning went out of control immediately and the pilot had no time to initiate a distress call before he ejected. This was the first recorded ejection from a British aircraft travelling faster than sound. The Martin Baker seat's barometric release separated the pilot at 10,000 ft, and he made a parachute descent into the uninviting waters below. He was to spend the next 28 hours in

Left *Lightning T 5 of 226 OCU Colishall at Lakenheath in 1970* (R.L. Ward).

Below *The second T 4 prototype which was originally known as the P 11. It carried the brunt of T 4 development after the loss, very early in the programme, of the first aircraft* (BAe).

Above *A T 4 of 226 OCU. This was the first T 4 to be delivered to the LCS at Middleton St George in 1962* (Peter March).

Below *The prototype T 4 XL628 at Farnborough on September 12 1959. This is the aircraft from which test pilot Johnny Squier ejected over the Irish Sea on October 1 1959 when the fin collapsed* (R. L. Ward).

Bottom *The wider front fuselage of the T 5 is very apparent in this head-on shot of an RAE aircraft* (RAE).

this hostile environment, seeing search and rescue aircraft pass over him without seeing his dinghy or the distress flares he fired. Eventually the exhausted pilot managed to paddle ashore using pieces of driftwood as makeshift paddles.

The loss of the aircraft after only 94 flights, during which it had accumulated 40 hours 51 minutes flying time, put the full load of development flying for the T 4 on to *XL629*, which had made its first flight two days before the loss of the first machine. On November 19, 'Bee' Beamont and Dizzy de Villiers had a shock in *XL629*, when the canopy parted company with the aircraft during the take-off run. The flight was immediately aborted without damage to either the aircraft or crew. This particular T 4 went on to complete the test programme and, after 187 hours flying, was passed to the Empire Test Pilots' School at Farnborough, arriving there on May 13 1966. It subsequently moved to Boscombe Down on December 20 1967 and in 1981 was still located there as gate guardian.

The first production T 4 was *XM966*, one of a batch of 20 ordered by the RAF, which made its first flight on July 15 1960. This particular aircraft, together with *XM967*, were never used by the RAF and were both converted to T 5 standard, the former having the distinction of being the first production T 4 and the second prototype T 5 to fly. It also had another distinction in that, like the original P 11 (*XL628*), it was lost over the Irish Sea on July 22 1965 when the fin failed. On this occasion both pilots, J. Dell and G. Elkington ejected safely and did not spend as long as their colleague Johnny Squier had in taking an unexpected 'dip'.

Of the 20 T 4s produced, 18 served with the RAF, either at the Lightning OCU or with first-line squadrons. Five were destroyed in crashes and two were purchased back by the BAC for use on the Saudi Arabia (Magic Carpet) contract. It is also of interest to note that *XM968* was used as a chase aircraft for the ill-fated TSR2 at both Boscombe Down and Warton. The second version of the two-seater was the T 5 which was equivalent to the F 3 in equipment and shape, although of course the forward fuselage was widened in the same way as the T 4.

As already mentioned, two T 4s were converted to basic T 5 standards at Filton and *XM967* made the first T 5 flight on March 29 1962 with Jimmy Dell at the controls. The first production T 5 to fly was, in fact, the second airframe of a batch of 20, *XS417*, which Jimmy took into the air for the first time on July 17 1964. Like the T 4, the new version was also designed to have a full operational role and was used in this capacity. An unusual aspect of the T 5 was that the throttles for the right-hand seat were on the right-hand side of the cockpit. This arrangement resulted in the pilot occupying this seat — usually the instructor — flying left handed, an unusual situation for a fighter pilot. Those who regularly instructed (and still do) on the T 5 quickly became adept at what is a very unnatural way of flying a high-performance aircraft.

The aircraft was issued to the Lightning OCU and operational squadrons in exactly the same way as its predecessor and continues to serve with the LTF and Nos 5 and 11 Sqns at Binbrook in 1983. There were in fact 22 T 5s built, the last two, *XV328* and *329*, being replacements for *XS453* and *XS460*. The first of the latter two crashed on June 1 1966 and the second was bought by the BAC from the Ministry of Defence for use on the Saudi contract, thus becoming the first T 55 export trainer. Of the 22 T 5s built, 21 served with the RAF and of these only three have been lost in accidents. The six Saudi and two Kuwaiti T 55s were fitted with the larger ventral tank and cambered wing of the F 6, which gave them increased range and performance, something that would no doubt have been an asset to the RAF units who operated the T 4s and T 5s. The last operational T 4s were used by Nos 19 and 92 Sqns in Germany, ultimately ending their days as decoys or fire-practice aircraft.

The small ventral tank of the T 4 is shown to advantage as XM997 rolls on to its back for the camera aircraft (MoD).

Above *Built as a T 4, XM967 was modified to T 5 configuration for development work* (BAe).

Below *This pleasing shot of the T 5 prototype clearly shows how the fuselage was increased in width to accommodate the second crew member* (BAe).

Chapter 6

The Lightning in service

During the period January 17–March 3 1958, three RAF pilots from the Central Fighter Establishment carried out a total of 16 flights from Warton to evaluate the Lightning. The aircraft used were *XA847*, the third prototype but first P 1B, *XA856*, the fifth prototype, fitted with production power controls, and the original P 1A *WG760*. The P 1B *XA847* bore the brunt of this initial evaluation by service pilots, flying a total of 13 flights; six of these were familiarisation and seven were sortie profiles. *XA856* was flown twice to give familiarisation to Wing Commanders James and Coulthard, and Wing Commander James flew *WG760*, by now with the cambered leading edge, on one occasion, to give him experience of the full-span, cambered leading edge. These two pilots, together with Flt Lt Carr, flew *XA847* with and without the ventral tank, at all-up weights of from 28,600 to 30,900 lb and at speeds up to Mach 1.5. The high Mach number was achieved in the operational profile flown by the three men; this profile included a cruise to 28,000 ft, followed by a maximum reheat climb to 36,000 ft, 2.5 g turns with minimum reheat, then an energy climb to 48,000 ft and a deceleration and descent at Mach 0.9. No doubt their enthusiasm for the aircraft was conveyed back to their fellow pilots at the CFE who took delivery of three late production aircraft, *XG334–336*, in December 1959.

The Air Fighting Development Squadron, which was part of the CFE, had the job of evaluating the Lightning for service use, and devising operational parameters for service pilots. The home of the CFE was RAF Coltishall, which was one of the airfields situated on the eastern side of Great Britain, earmarked for improvements, including an extension to the main runway, that would enable it to accept the new supersonic interceptor. Sharing the airfield with the CFE was one of the RAF's most famous fighter squadrons, No 74, whose history dated back to the First World War and whose record during the Second World War was second to none. No 74 was named as the first unit to be equipped with the Lightning, so as the AFDS operated their new mounts, the pilots of 74, who at that time were flying Hunters, had a grandstand preview of what was in store for them. During May 1960, the AFDS took their new aircraft to Leconfield where they were participants in that year's air-defence exercise, during which they achieved a very encouraging success rate. The following month, the first of 74's initial batch of 12 F 1 Lightnings was delivered, this aircraft being *XM165*, which had been ferried from Warton to AFDS at Leconfield by Jimmy Dell on the 29th of the month, then flown to Coltishall — when runway repairs were completed — by Flt Lt Bruce Hopkins. It arrived in a five-aircraft formation, led by Wing Commander David Simmons. Incidentally, this was the first occasion that five RAF Lightnings were photographed in the air together in formation. The three other aircraft were flown by Sqn Ldr Frank Babst, Flt Lt Peter Collins and Flt Lt Ken Goodwin, all of AFDS. This aircraft therefore has the distinction of being the first Lightning to serve with an operational squadron; it was later passed to

226 OCU and ended its days at 33 MU, where it was scrapped in October 1966. Conversion from the Hunter started immediately and was overseen by the CFE's Lightning Conversion Unit (LCU). The Lightning was a tremendous leap forward in terms of performance, having twice the speed of the Hunter and a far greater rate of climb. To underline the difference and the way the pilots had to adjust, it is worth considering just one example.

At this time there were no two-seat Lightnings in service, so the embryo pilot commenced his conversion by being taken on his initial sorties with an experienced Lightning pilot in a two-seat Hunter; such was the margin of performance of the Lightning, that to enable the two aircraft to fly in formation at operational height, the Lightning had to give the Hunter a 28,000 ft start from take-off. The aircraft also introduced a new concept to aerial interception, for it had been designed from the outset as a completely integrated weapons' system and was therefore capable of accurately identifying, tracking and destroying enemy aircraft without any visual contact. In addition to Aden cannons, similar to those used in the Hunter, it was also armed with two de Havilland Firestreak missiles mounted on either side of the cockpit.

The Firestreak was the production version of the Blue Jay, mentioned earlier in the text, and first entered service with the RAF during 1958, when it was fitted to twin-seat Javelin fighters. These had equivalent interception capability to that of the Lightning, although this had not been designed into them originally. The Javelin's Firestreak armament and radar were fitted as a modification as their original armament had only been the conventional 30 mm Aden cannon. The Firestreak was an air-to-air missile using infra-red passive-homing guidance which, when fired, was boosted to supersonic speed by its own internal rocket motor; it then locked on to its target and followed it continuously until contact was made. The Ferranti airborne-interception radar, mounted in the nose cone, allowed the pilot to search above and below the horizon until the target was located.

He then manually initiates the 'lock-on' function, which enables the radar to track the target automatically and prevents contact from being lost. Radar information is processed through an on-board computer and steering information thus provided to the pilot on his attack sight enables him to close to missile-firing range. If the target attempts to carry out evading action, the Lightning's radar detects this and compensates for it. Should a target be flying at transonic speeds the aircraft's superiority is such that it can overtake at a rate of one mile for every two covered by the target. Missile range is far greater than that of the aircraft's cannons and when a target is within such range, the homing head of the missile(s) automatically locks on to the target and the pilot is instructed electronically to fire.

The new fighter and its armament presented a challenge to 74 Squadron, whose commanding officer at this time was Sqn Ldr J.F.G. Howe, but, with the help of the pilots of the AFDS, the squadron soon began to work up to an efficiency level that enabled them to fly four Lightnings in a formation display on the public days of the 1960 Farnborough air show. During July and August 1960, Lightning F 1s *XM139–144*, *XM146-147*, *XM164* and *166* were added to the squadron, *XM167* bringing the strength to 12 by September 26 and *XM145* completing the initial complement of 13 when it was delivered on May 14 1962. In January 1961, the squadron recorded over 100 hours of Lightning flying in a month for the first time, an achievement which had eluded them until then because of poor weather and low serviceability as ground crews became used to their new charges.

The latter is not intended to imply criticism, since the Lightning was a complicated aircraft and those responsible for servicing its airframe, engines, instruments, radar and electronic equipment, had a task equally as daunting as those converting from the Hunter

Above *Pilots of No 74 Squadron line up for a company publicity photograph with a F 1 (BAe).*

Below *A Wattisham TFF Lightning F 1 (XM147) which served with AFDS, 74 Squadron and 56 Squadron as well as the Binbrook and Leuchars TFFs. It lost its fin in flight during January 1970 but was landed safely and repaired at 60 MU. It was photographed at Alconbury in October 1972 (R.L. Ward).*

Above *Another view of* XM139, *one of the original production-batch Lightnings, which was at one time the RAF's Fighter Display Aircraft* (R.L. Ward).

to fly it. It says a lot for the dedication of the ground crews and the long hours put in by them, that the squadron should pass the 100-hour landmark in a month not noted for providing ideal flying weather. During the same month No 74 Squadron's designation — of a short-range, day-fighter squadron — was changed to that of a night and all-weather unit, underlining the new role that the Lightning now enabled fighter squadrons to adopt.

On February 28 all 74's Lightnings were grounded, due to a serious potential fire hazard being discovered between the ventral tank and No 1 engine jet-pipe. By March 2 the aircraft were operational again, a temporary solution having been achieved by removing the ventral tanks. This enabled flying to continue but the aircraft's duration, already limited, was even more curtailed, though by the 18th of the month a manufacturer's modification (ST1/20) had been carried out and the tanks were refitted. The following month, the squadron was able to use its aircraft for the first time in a military exercise, named Matador, on April 19, during which the Lightnings were credited with ten 'kills', a rate that delighted the pilots. Being the first RAF squadron to be equipped with the Lightning, No 74 naturally became an attraction to not only the aviation press but also the more wide-ranging national daily papers.

Although there was an element of truth in the stories published in the daily newspapers, a certain amount of journalistic licence was inevitable so that the imagination of the layman could be captured and held. The less knowledgeable might be forgiven for thinking that all pilots selected for the Lightning were 'supermen' with many thousands of hours to their credit. Initially pilots with a minimum of 1,000 hours on fast jets *were* selected for the Lightning squadrons, but this criterion did not last long and the handling of the new fighter soon allowed pilots straight from their advanced-flight training schools, with perhaps 50 hours fast-jet experience, to be posted to a Lightning unit. Such pilots were of course subjected to a continuation of their training at squadron level and it was some time before they were fully fledged, operational members of the squadron.

Graduating from the Hunter made it necessary to introduce certain steps to ease the transition between two aircraft of such startlingly different performance. This started with a five-day, aviation-medicine course, during which pilots were taught the problems which could be encountered during high-level flying. They were also fitted with their

Top XM140, *a Lightning F 1, delivered to No 74 Squadron on August 2 1960. It later served with No 111 Squadron and was scrapped in 1966* (Peter March).

Above *A four-aircraft formation, flown by No 74 Squadron* (Peter March).

flying clothing, including a special pressure-helmet, which then, in 1960, was only used by crews flying the PR 9 Canberra. Other lectures on the aircraft's systems and handling were given and during this time about eleven hours were spent on the Lightning simulator, after which the first solo, bringing with it a taste of the acceleration provided by the two Avons, was undertaken.

The pilots revelled in having a machine which, as Sqn Ldr Howe was quick to point out, could outfight anything in the American Century-series fighters and put Great Britain back in the front line of high-speed interceptors. What of course was not over-publicised was the fact that the American aircraft referred to had been in squadron service for some time and were available in far greater quantities; nonetheless, none of these fighters remain in use today whereas the Lighting is still a formidable opponent, albeit in the twilight of its career.

The Farnborough Air Show 1961 saw 74 Squadron replace the four-aircraft formation of the previous year with nine machines and in 1962, under their new commanding officer, Sqn Ldr Peter Botterill, the unit became the RAF's leading aerobatic team. Known as 'The Tigers', each aircraft sported a black spine and fin, and on the latter the

Above *Seven F 1s of No 74 Squadron fly a neat formation, soon after the squadron was equipped with the Lightning* (Peter March).

Below *F 1s of No 74 Squadron show off their Diamond Nine formation during an early Lightning aerobatic display* (Peter March).

squadron's famous tiger's head was painted, though the only other concessions to colour were the black and yellow markings either side of the fuselage roundel. For the 1962 display season, the squadron flew a seven-aircraft formation team, which started its display with a slow fly-past in formation with gear and flaps down, after thrilling the crowd with a full reheat take-off. The formation then climbed into a steep turn followed by a wing-over and a box roll, changing into another wing-over which became a line astern as it progressed, and ended with the aircraft in echelon starboard. Other features included a bomb burst, change rolls and a spectacular two-way break over the airfield.

The Lightning may not have appeared to have been the best aircraft for an aerobatic team, but as Sqn Ldr Botterill explained at the time, the average speed was limited to 400 knots, which enabled the formation to stay within the confines of most airfields and the aircraft were also constantly turning to ensure observation of this important criterion. The aircraft's speed and power were not liabilities in such manoeuvres, but could be introduced to initiate a spectacular climb or change in attitude guaranteed to thrill any crowd. The team received many accolades during 1962, which included displays in Sweden, Norway and at RAF Upavon to commemorate 50 years of British military aviation.

Both 74 and 92 Squadrons, the latter to receive Lightnings in late 1962, had earned for themselves reputations as expert practitioners of stunning formation aerobatics and, during the 1962 Farnborough display, they combined to field a formation of 16 all-blue Hunters from 92 and 10 Lightnings from 74. Perhaps this helped to restore some of the balance of friendly rivalry between the two squadrons which had reached a peak in July 1961 when 92 Squadron, which was then the official RAF Fighter Command aerobatic team, had been away from their base in Leconfield and 74 had given their first display with Lightnings at this location during a visit of the Queen Mother! Formation aerobatics was and, indeed, still is a vital and demanding task, and while it is essential that it is mastered by every aspiring fighter pilot, it is equally important that everyday efficiency is maintained. Thus although 74 were the official Fighter Command aerobatic team, they still kept their role as a front-line fighting unit, very conscious of their responsibility.

During aerobatic displays the pilots were constantly experiencing turns in the order of 3–4g, not a particularly high figure as far as the Lightning was concerned, but enough to make the pilots thankful for the comfort provided by their anti-g suits. On June 16 1962, as No 74 worked up its display, one pilot experienced 'stick jamming' in conditions of fairly high g loading. He returned to Coltishall and an investigation revealed that a balance-weight attached to the lower end of the control column could foul the aircraft structure beneath the cockpit floor when 2g was exceeded. An immediate restriction limiting the aircraft to within 2g parameters was introduced, but a modification programme was quickly instituted, which solved the problem and resulted in all restrictions being removed.

The F 1s used by 74 Squadron generated a great deal of interest within the Indian Air Force and, during 1961, it looked very much as though 12 aircraft would be exported to that country; there was also a strong possibility that most of them would be the squadron's aircraft, thus enabling them to receive the F 1A as replacements. However, the deal eventually fell through and 74 continued to operate the F 1 — the only operational squadron to do so — until April 1964, when it started to be phased out, eventually being totally replaced on the unit by the greatly improved Mk 3. By that time, a very high level of efficiency had been reached, an example of this being on March 23 1963 when a Fighter Command alert was called.

This came at 15.02 hours, at which time the squadron had only two F 1s on readiness. During the following 2½ hours, eight aircraft were scrambled, in other words 80 per cent of the available serviceable aircraft. Quite an indication of the peaks achieved by the air and ground crews in working up a completely new aircraft in a comparatively short space of time! Another sign of the level of efficiency and dedication to every aspect of operational flying, came a month later on April 26, when Flt Lt T.J. Burns experienced a total control failure in *XM142* and ejected off Cromer. This was one of the cleanest ejections experienced by the squadron and was carried out in textbook style, the pilot receiving no injuries and being recovered from his unscheduled dip in record time.

In July 1963, seven of No 74's F 1 Lightnings departed to the Lightning Operational Conversion Unit (OCU) at Middleton St George (now Tyne-Tees Airport), where they joined the T 4s. After passing through 60 MU at Leconfield, the F 1s emerged with their fins painted in a distinctive red and white scheme and with the last three figures of the serial number forward of the nose roundel. The fins also carried the cross-and-sword badge of No 145 Squadron, which was the 'shadow' unit identity given to the OCU. The seven aircraft were replaced on 74 Squadron with F 1s taken from the AFDS, among which was *XM134*, the first production machine, which eventually also found its way to the OCU.

In February 1964, No 226 OCU moved into Coltishall, previously the home of No 74, this unit now being located at Leuchars to re-equip with the F 3. As service aircraft from other Lightning units were replaced, they were routed to the OCU or into store with 33 MU at Lyneham. This unit was in the process of being closed down, all Lightning major servicing becoming the responsibility of 60 MU at Leconfield. Before finally closing, 33 MU scrapped several F 1s including *XM140, 141, 143, 146, 165, 166* and *167*, but also transferred several aircraft to Leconfield. It was whilst preparing one of these machines, *XM135*, that the commanding officer of the unit wrote a chapter of aviation and RAF history unlikely ever to be repeated; namely his involuntary flight in the aircraft.

This incident occurred on Friday, July 22 1966, the 'pilot' being a 40-year-old engineering officer, Wing Commander Walter 'Taffy' Holden. The Lightning was being prepared as a supersonic target for Fighter Command and on its first test flight the standy-by invertor came on just after Flt Lt J. Reynolds, a Boscombe Down Handling Squadron pilot, had become airborne. This incident happened on June 29, and was reported by the pilot; a full investigation revealed no fault and all checks proved satisfactory, but on the second air test exactly the same thing happened. Once again, the fault could not be located and once again it had recurred just after take-off; another investigation failed to locate or diagnose the fault, so a decision was taken to isolate the two parts of the stand-by invertor and test them in turn. Flt Lt Reynolds was not available to carry out the necessary taxi tests but briefed Wing Commander Holden of the maximum rpm he could expect the brakes to hold, as well as certain cockpit precautions.

Prior to having *XM135* towed to the runway, Holden carried out a full cockpit check and acquainted himself with the engine-running procedures, not only on this aircraft but also on *XM176*, which was another aircraft being prepared by the MU for target-facility work. The Lightning had its canopy removed, to enable additional test wiring to be instal-led, the ejection seat was disarmed with the safety pins in place and the undercarriage ground-locks were in position. Since the fault had appeared on three occasions just after the brakes had been released for take-off, it was Holden's intention to open the engines up to 80–90 per cent their full power on the brakes, release them, then immediately close the throttles and stop.

The sun hovered in a clear blue sky and the heat of the July day caused that characteristic shimmer often seen on airfields, as the Lightning was positioned at the end of Lyneham's north/south runway 36/18, which Air Traffic Control had closed because of the tests, Holden was strapped into the aircraft, but did not fit the leg restraints. He ran through the cockpit checks from the pilot's notes which he had with him and a further check was carried out by a charge-hand engine fitter, before the access ladder was removed and the twin Avons ignited. Three test runs were made which used less than 100 yds of the runway so Air Traffic Control, having observed these, switched the perimeter track lights crossing runway 36 to green. On the fourth run, the Wing Commander inadvertently pushed the throttles into the reheat position and the aircraft immediately accelerated — his first reaction was that the throttles had jammed. He quickly realised that this was not the case, but by this time the speed was building up at an alarming rate and he became aware of a vehicle crossing the runway; at the same time he also recalled the proximity of the village of Bradenstoke at the end of the runway now being rapidly devoured by the speeding Lightning. With only 2,000 ft of runway left there was no way that the aircraft could be stopped, so the only course of action left was to take off. Air Traffic Control realised what had happened but, as Holden was not wearing a helmet and the radio equipment was not switched on, there was nothing they could do to help him, except clear the Lyneham circuit of traffic and alert the emergency services.

Unable to eject, the Wing Commander had no choice other than to attempt to land the Lightning, a daunting prospect since, although he had flown solo many years before in a Harvard, his only experience of a jet was a one-hour trip in a Javelin T 3 on Nov 15 1962 and this had not included landings or take-offs with his hands on the controls. Gingerly, he turned the aircraft into the Lyneham circuit to line up with the duty runway (07), but poor co-ordination of airspeed, height and runway alignment resulted in the first attempt being aborted. Two further efforts resulted in the same decision being taken; of the many problems being faced, not the least was the need to keep the airspeed below the safety

Below *An F 3 of 226 OCU in the markings of No 145 Squadron photographed at Farnborough in 1970* (author's collection).

minimum with gear and flaps down, and this clearly exacerbated the problems of landing. Holden decided that the 12-kt wind, which was blowing from 020°, might enable him to make a better approach and landing, with less risk to life, if he tried runway 25. Keeping two Britannias that were 'holding' just off the circuit in sight, he changed direction onto his new heading, hoping that Air Traffic Control would become aware of his intentions.

His preoccupation with speed rather than altitude and turns that were marginally too steep, and executed at too low a height, caused much consternation to those watching from the ground. The first pass at the new runway failed because of the high speed and altitude, but the second attempt was successful and the Lightning touched down at something over 160 kts with its nose held high. The tail-skid hit the runway hard and in so doing damaged the braking 'chute cables, though this was not realised until the pilot released the 'chute only to have it fall away without providing any retardation. Heavy application of the brakes and the uphill gradient of the runway brought the Lightning to a halt about 100 yd from the end of the runway. The total flight time was 12 minutes, which seemed like a lifetime to the engineering officer at the controls.

He commented later that his salvation was due to his flying experience, very limited as it may have been, and the meagre information he had gleaned from the pilot's notes which he had read prior to boarding *XM135*. It is also interesting to note that the notes stayed on board the aircraft, despite the absence of the canopy, and the 'pilot' reported that, despite not wearing a helmet, the slipstream and its noise were tolerable. The aircraft, which had served with 74 Squadron during 1963, was repaired and used by the Target Facilities Flight at Leuchars, and as a general 'hack' by 60 MU, before being retired to the Imperial War Museum collection at Duxford on November 20 1974 with 1,343 flying hours to its credit, including those remarkable 12 minutes.

Below *A Target Facilities Flight F 1A photographed at RAF Binbrook during March 1973. At this time the aircraft, XM181, was approaching its twelfth year of service, which had started in September 1961 with No 111 Squadron (MoD).*

Above and below *Lightning F 1A XM192 on gate-guard duty at RAF Wattisham. This aircraft flew 2,186 hours with No 111 Squadron, the Binbrook and Wattisham Target Facilities Flights and 226 OCU. It carries the markings of No 111 Squadron, and is now instructional airframe 8413M.*

Above *An early production F 1 serving with the TFF at Wattisham in 1973. In 1969 this aircraft was the official RAF Fighter Display Aircraft and was flown at the SBAC Display Farnborough and the Paris Air show* (MoD).

Below *XM139 an F 1 of the Wattisham TFF streams its braking 'chute as it lands at Chivenor. Note the absence of cable ducts which distinguishes the F 1 from the F 1A* (R.L. Ward).

Below *The F 1 was used by Target Facility Flights when it was retired from squadron service. XM139 is seen here serving with the Wattisham TFF, in 1972. This aircraft was, in 1970, the official RAF fighter-display aircraft and was flown by Flight Lieutenant Russ Pengelly at the 1970 and 1972 SBAC displays, and the 1971 Paris Air Show. It became instructional airframe 8411M and was in use at Wattisham, in 1981* (R.L. Ward).

Top *Starboard side of the Binbrook TFF* XM181. *The unit's lion badge on the fin is blue on a white background* (MoD).
Above *Lightning F 1A* (XM173) *of No 56 Squadron in the colourful markings of that unit. This aircraft also served with 226 OCU and was the gate guardian at Bentley Priory in 1981* (Peter March).

Some of the F 1 aircraft like *XM135* were being converted by 33 MU for use as target-facility aircraft, thus fulfilling a need that had become evident as early as October 1961. At this time 111 Squadron, which had started to re-equip with Lightnings in April, noted that the target-facility-flight (TFF) Canberras (provided by 85 Squadron) could not operate satisfactorily in this role above 45,000 ft; the answer was to use a Lightning but, although this was not an ideal aircraft since it presented a poor radar picture, a greater problem was its unavailability, as all new aircraft were required for squadron use. However, in 1966, the AFDS (which was renamed Fighter Command Trials Unit on January 31), received two F 1s, *XM164* and *XM137*, which they successfully evaluated in this role. When the trials' unit was disbanded, the two aircraft remained at Binbrook where they formed the station's target-facility flight. Other such flights, usually with two or three aircraft, were formed at Wattisham and Leuchars where they operated under their own commanding officers as independent units.

The TFF Lightnings operated as high-speed targets, simulating every possible type of deception and manoeuvre which might be tried by a hostile aircraft. Although attached to one of the wings on the parent base, the TFFs operated as separate units, having their own pilots and ground crews. They also adopted their own markings which invariably included the station badge and, at Wattisham, the aircraft were named after cartoon characters, these being Felix, Jinx and Korky, a trio of well-known mischievous cats. The spirit of the crews was always high and some TFFs boasted a higher serviceability and flying rate (in proportion to aircraft operated) than the squadrons they served.

With 74 Squadron well established with their F 1s, it became the turn of two equally famous fighter squadrons to re-equip with the Lightning. The first of these was No 56, which could trace its formation back to June 8 1916 and its pedigree through both world wars, and included two air VCs among its former pilots, these being Capt Albert Ball and Capt James McCudden. Changing their Meteor 8s for the ill-fated Vickers Supermarine Swift in February 1954, the squadron had many traumatic experiences in operating the first swept-wing interceptor to enter RAF service, before it was withdrawn and they were re-equipped with Hunters. In the same way that the Swift had represented a considerable advance over the Meteor, the Lightning now made the Hunter look quite pedestrian, but no doubt this was gratefully accepted by the squadron pilots.

The first F 1A to be delivered to 56 arrived in the hands of Peter Hillwood on December 14 1960. This was *XM172*, which had made its maiden flight on October 10 1960 and was destined to survive the rigours of squadron service, becoming instructional airframe *8427M* and Coltishall's gate guardian. Between December and June, five new aircraft arrived thus putting the proposed delivery schedule about two weeks behind the target date, though this did not impair the unit's work-up to operational status which took place at Wattisham and, later, Coltishall, during a period when the runway at the former base was undergoing essential maintenance work.

In June 1961, Flt Lts J. Swart and J. Farwell took Lightnings *XM182* and *XM177* to USAF open days at Bentwaters and Mildenhall, and both recorded how gratifying it was to fly an RAF fighter that had a better performance than the current USAF fighters on display.

The fitting of the in-flight refuelling probe to the F 1A went a long way to helping with the problem of short duration, which was a serious shortcoming of the F 1 and, indeed, not really overcome as far as internal tankage was concerned until the evolution of the large ventral tank for the F 6. It fell to 56 Squadron to conduct intensive trials of air-to-air refuelling. Two aircraft were able to carry out the first overseas flight-refuelling exercise on July 23 1962, when they flew non-stop from their base to Akrotiri in 4 hrs 22 minutes, refuelling from Valiant tankers of Nos 90 and 214 Squadrons. Three months later a general press release was issued in which it was reported that on Thursday, October 4 1962, four Lightnings of No 56 Squadron were to fly non-stop to Cyprus on the first routine training flight, thus confirming that sufficient progress had been made to make this 2,000-mile flight, of some 4½ hours, something well within the capacity of the average squadron pilot. The four men who took the Lightnings to Cyprus were Flt Lts A.C. Curry, R.J. Manning, B.J. Cheater and Flying Officer D.G Adam, and those who handled the aircraft for the return flight on October 9 were Flt Lts N.D. McEwen, R. Cloke, E.E. Jones and M.J. Moore.

These early trials by 56 Squadron laid the foundations of the techniques and methods used by RAF Lightning squadrons, and became an essential part of their training when deployments to Cyprus, Malta, Singapore and other overseas bases became common for the Lightning.

'Treble One' squadron, which shared Wattisham with 56, earned a reputation for itself as a unit with a difference when it came to aerobatics, the famous loop by 22 Hunters at the SBAC display in 1958 still being talked about and to date unsurpassed. This unit began to receive its Lightning F 1As in April 1961, the first two to arrive being *XM184* and *XM186*, which were flown in from Warton by Flt Lt Goodwin and Sqn Ldr Robertson on the 13th. Since it was a pilot of 111 who had flown a Hurricane from London to Edinburgh in 1938 to establish a speed record between the cities, which was broken in 1955 by a Hunter F 4 of the same unit at 717 mph, it was perhaps a little surprising that an early attempt to better this, using the Lightning, was not undertaken.

But training was of greater importance than record breaking, so it is not really too surprising that the unit buckled down to the task of becoming operational. Some of their early tasks were parallel to those carried out by 56 on flight refuelling, with this squadron also undertaking overseas trials to Germany, Malta and Cyprus. The extended range provided by this technique was a bonus much appreciated by Lightning pilots, who for a long time continued to be critical of the aircraft's poor built-in fuel capacity. Even when the F 3 started to arrive with the squadrons, duration was still a problem and flight refuelling a necessity. This is highlighted by a comment made by Sqn Ldr Maish of 74 Squadron who on March 26 1965 took his F 3 to Upper Heyford for in-flight refuelling trials with a USAF KC135. These proved to be successful and the pilot said that he hoped it was a foretaste of things to come, though he might of course have been referring to the Green Shield trading stamps handed to him by the American crew of the tanker when it landed!*

By the end of June 1961, 111 squadron had nine Lightnings on strength despite the fact that on the 28th of the month one of its pilots, Flying Officer P.J. Ginger, had been forced to eject from *XM185* when he had trouble with the undercarriage. Once again, this was a perfect ejection with no injury to the pilot, with the aircraft falling near Rattlesden, and did not deplete the unit's aircraft complement since *XM185* belonged to 56 Squadron and at the time was on loan to 111! By September 29, Treble One was declared fully operational, the transition from the subsonic Hunter to the Lightning having taken just six months. October started badly with all aircraft being grounded due to the necessity to carry out a works-notified modification. This was the lagging and separation of all closely routed hydraulic pipes. Mid-November saw the aircraft back in full service but, once again, flying was curtailed in December, not this time due to any problems with the aircraft but the need to help the USAF. Two officers and 75 airmen were sent to USAF base Wethersfield to patrol the perimeter during a CND demonstration that lasted three and a half days; effectively, all the campaign succeeded in doing was to keep part of one of the country's Lightning squadrons grounded.

1963 saw No 56 Squadron named as Fighter Command's aerobatic team, taking over from No 92 which was stood-down to re-equip with the F 2 Lightning. Known as the 'Firebirds', because of the Phoenix insignia in their badge, 56 painted their aircraft with a red fin, spine and wing leading edges, but retained the red/white chequered nose markings. They gave many scintillating displays during the year, but lost two aircraft during a practice formation fly-past and bomb-burst over Wattisham on June 6. Flt Lt Mike Cook, flying *XM179*, collided with *XM174*. Cook ejected but, in so doing, broke his neck and sadly is now paralysed and confined to a wheelchair. The wreckage of his aircraft fell at Great Bricett, while the other aircraft landed safely. Oddly enough, the latter was destroyed some five years later when its pilot ejected in Scotland when the aircraft was with the Leuchars target-facility flight.

These were stamps issued by companies against purchases and were very popular at this time. Garages often vied with each other to give the most stamps against purchases of petrol.

Above XR771, *'C', of No 56 Squadron at Wattisham on April 9 1976* (R.L. Ward).

Below *The Lightning is a BIG aeroplane! This airman lends scale to the intake of an F 6 of No 56 Squadron* (R.L. Ward).

Above *A Victor K2 tanker of No 232 OCU RAF Marham refuels two F 6s of No 11 Squadron.* (Peter Stevenson, MoD).

Below *This F 2, XN794, seen in the markings of No 19 Squadron, was one of the airframes not converted to F 2A standard. It became instructional airframe 8349M* (Peter March).

During this period of work-up with the Lightning, the two squadrons based at Wattisham worked very closely together, in many cases following parallel paths. Although, in 1965, Treble One was to form a Lightning aerobatic team with twelve F 3 aircraft, it was content to let the Firebirds take the glory during 1963 and 1964, during which time one of its tasks was to train with the Lightning for the ground-attack role. Its potential development in this role had been foreseen and, during detachments to El Adem in Libya, the unit practised not only air-to-air firing with cannons and 2-in rockets in place of Firestreaks, but also air-to-ground gunnery when two 30 mm Adens replaced the Firestreaks.

Most of the firings took place at Mach .95 at 36,000 ft, but in one session at least one pass was made at Mach 1.4 at 48,000 ft. During this particular session, all aircraft used only the two ventral cannons, apart from one occasion on which one aircraft used four. During this period, flight-refuelling exercises were still of paramount importance and Treble One carried out successful compatibility trials by taking on fuel from Fleet Air Arm Sea Vixen tankers.

With Nos 74, 56 and 111 Squadrons well established with Lightning F 1s and F 1As, it became the turn of another long-established squadron, No 19, to convert to the supersonic fighter. This squadron, together with No 92, comprised the Leconfield Hunter Wing and could trace its origins to September 1915. It was the first RAF squadron to receive the Spitfire in August 1938, and no doubt similar enthusiasm awaited the arrival of its first Lightning in October 1962. With the T 4 now well established at the Lightning OCU at Middleton St George, it became policy to allocate at least one T 4 to all operational squadrons. Consequently, to enable No 19 to start its conversion course, the first aircraft it received was T 4 *XM988*, which arrived from 229 OCU on October 29, having been delivered to Middleton St George on the 12th of the month. It was accepted by the squadron on October 31 and taken on to its strength on November 15, by which time three more T 4s, *XM994, XM995* and *XM972*, had arrived. The squadron got off to a frustrating start with *XM994* developing a hydraulic leak on its acceptance flight on December 10, this being traced to the incorrect assembly of a component and, during this check, a fuel leak was also discovered and sadly this was attributed to the same cause.

The first F 2, *XN775*, was delivered to Leconfield on December 17 and on its acceptance flight on January 10 1963, a fault was found in the reheat system. Only the day before the units second F 2, *XN778*, had been diverted to Finningley, following the indication of a fire in No 1 engine during an air test. However, these really were minor problems and the squadron strength was up to its complement of 12 F 2s and a T 4 during March, by which time three of the original T 4s had been returned to the OCU. The F2 was a notable improvement over the F 1A, its fully variable reheat and partial OR 946 flight instrumentation giving it an edge over the earlier version. No 19 Squadron became operational with its new mounts during March 1963, much of its early flying having been the gaining of experience in operating their new supersonic interceptors and adapting to an all-weather role. In July 1963, 19 Squadron achieved 280 sorties for the month, giving a total of 216.30 hours, their best to date with the Lightning. By October, this had reached 375 sorties, totalling just over 300 hours, which included 98 practice interceptions carried out at supersonic speeds.

The inevitable flight-refuelling exercises commenced in January 1964, 19 Squadron's F 2s appearing with detachable probes under their port wings. At this time the unit's main responsibility was the preservation of the integrity of UK airspace and a pair of Lightnings was kept on alert in much the same way as they still are today, with only the title being changed, to Quick Reaction Alert (QRA). In-flight refuelling enabled aircraft to stay on station much longer, as well as enhancing overseas deployment. In June 1964, No 19 followed the example pioneered by No 56 with a deployment to Cyprus. Such was the success of this, and the confidence that the crews had in their aircraft, that the squadron's engineering officer was heard to remark on arrival in Cyprus, 'Well, since we have come this far successfully, why don't we hop across to Singapore for a day or two?' Prophetic words, but in the event, not for 19 Squadron. In 1965, the squadron was selected to take part in trials with the Victor K 1 tanker and, in the same year, won the coveted Dacre Trophy for the second time.

Sharing Leconfield with No 19 Squadron was No 92, which in 1954 had been one of two squadrons in Fighter Command to operate the North American F 86 Sabre, the other being No 66. Its association with No 19, as part of the Leconfield Hunter wing, continued with the Lightning, when it became the second and last RAF squadron to equip with this particular mark. The first F 2 to arrive with 92 was *XN727*, which was delivered by J. K. Isherwood on January 23 1963 and coded 'A'. This aircraft was used in conjunction with the T 4 in the same way as it had been by 19 to convert their pilots. The main body of F 2s began to arrive towards the end of March, starting with *XN783* which took over the 'A' code. Six more aircraft arrived in April and, by the end of June, the unit was at full strength, becoming operational before the end of the summer. The conversion from the Hunter to the Lightning, as far as 92 Squadron was concerned, proceeded smoothly although it was marred on April 27 when *XN785* 'C' crashed in attempting to land at a disused airfield, Hutton Cranswick, after a flight-refuelling exercise, Flying Officer Davey unfortunately being fatally injured.

In 1964, 92 Squadron became the official RAF aerobatic team and their blue-tailed Lightnings became as popular at air shows, including the SBAC show at Farnborough, as all other Lightning squadrons accorded this duty had been. But the main task for No 92 in 1964, as well as for No 19, was not aerobatics, but devotion to training for ground-attack work, which saw their aircraft mainly employed in a four-cannon configuration. This concentration, on ground attack, was aimed at perfecting an additional role to that of air interception, a new role that was seen as vitally important, especially in Germany, the future destination of the two squadrons.

No 19 was the first of the two units to depart for Germany, leaving Leconfield on September 23 under the command of Wing Commander Brian Cox, for Gütersloh. Its arrival in Germany was greeted with considerable enthusiasm, as the Lightning was the first supersonic aircraft to serve with the 2nd Tactical Air Force, with the display on arrival widely reported in the German press — one paper commenting that , '. . . it was formation flying the like of which has not been seen before'. 92 Squadron followed three months later, arriving at Geilenkirchen on December 29.

Below *A 92 Squadron F 2 gets airborne in a hurry at Leconfield. This aircraft was converted to F 2A standard in 1968 and returned to 92 Squadron* (Peter March).

Bottom *The F 2A of Wing Commander Barcilon (now Group Captain at Binbrook and still flying Lightnings), before dark green camouflage became a feature of German-based aircraft. The aircraft is XN781 of No 19 Squadron* (R.L. Ward).

Above *Two F 2As, of 92 Squadron get airborne in a hurry from RAF Gütersloh on April 26 1974* (R.L. Ward).

Below *A 19 Squadron F 2A, in the dark green, low-visibility scheme, transits at low level during a sortie from Gütersloh, 80 miles from the East German border* (MoD).

Bottom *A pair of Firestreak-armed Lightnings in their QRA alert shelter in Germany* (RAF Germany).

Above *The white-painted Firestreaks contrast against the dark green camouflage of this No 92 Squadron F 2A at readiness at Gütersloh* (MoD).

Both squadrons immediately slotted into their roles as an integral part of 2nd Allied Tactical Air Force, providing a vital part of the air defence of North-Western Europe. Battle flights were maintained at constant readiness and both units continued to perfect their dual roles of interception and ground attack. The pilots became very attached to the F 2s and many, who had previously experienced earlier marks, voted it the best Lightning they had flown. There were, of course, problems in the early days, not only in becoming acclimatised to the new aircraft and operational conditions, but also with teething difficulties such as fuel and hydraulic leaks. Although, as previously mentioned, the pilots took an instant liking to their new mounts, Flying Officer Wolff of 92 Squadron probably considered the attachment too endearing when, on November 22 1966, he was unable to open the canopy of his aircraft after landing and spent nearly two hours attached to *XN732* before being released by ground crew who removed the canopy. The fault was found to have been caused by a loose rivet head which jammed the 'shoot' bolts.

In February 1968, 92 Squadron joined 19 Squadron at Gütersloh and, soon after this, both units began to receive the Lightning F 2A. This greatly improved version of the F 2, with its F 6-type fin and large ventral tank, is still considered by many Lightning pilots to be the best of all marks. It was marginally lighter than the F 6, its engines did not get so hot and, in many other minor respects it was considered to be better. Even during a visit to Binbrook in 1983, where the last operational Lightnings serve, the author was told in no uncertain terms that the F 2A is *still* the ultimate Lightning.

The two German-based squadrons were destined to be the only units to receive the F 2A but, even at the time they started to take them on charge, there were very strong rumours that the McDonnell Douglas Phantom would be replacing the Lightning in RAF service before the seventies. In April 1967, 19 Squadron took their Lightnings to Bitburg where they had the opportunity to see USAF F 4s in operation and to give several American pilots an introduction to the Lightning via the unit's T 4. The Americans were very impressed by the British aircraft's rate of climb, but considered the pilot work-load rather high — another factor that will be mentioned later. One USAF pilot endeared himself to 19 Squadron when he described the Lightning's cockpit as 'kinda cosy'.

The first F 2A to be delivered to 19 Squadron was *XN789*, which arrived in January 15 1968. Of the 44 F 2s built, 28 were fully converted to F 2A standard and these all went to the two German-based squadrons.

Situated only 80 miles from the East German border, the two Gütersloh-based squadrons played a vital part in NATO's European defence line, their ability to outperform all others in the quick-reaction, interception role being a crucial element in defence against a possible attack from the east. The squadrons' Lightnings had the task of defending the airspace between the East and West, and preserving the sterile zone into which no Allied aircraft are allowed to venture. The rapid scramble time, the ability to climb very quickly and the fast acceleration to high speed, made the Lightning an ideal weapon for this task, and two aircraft, known to NATO as the Interceptor Alert Force, were continuously ready in purpose-built hangars located adjacent to the runway at Gütersloh.

Air and ground crews constantly rehearsed operations under warlike conditions, these covering every scenario from a nuclear attack to the launch of chemical warfare. Such a state of readiness required a very high level of aircraft serviceability if it was to be a viable deterrent but, in 1971, 92 Squadron had many problems to contend with. The most serious of these was the acquisition of spares, a situation not entirely unknown to Lightning units, since in July 1967 a UK-based squadron had reported its efficiency to be seriously impaired by the absence of vital parts.

Above *An F 2A of 19 Squadron showing off the new toned-down, green camouflage, just after it was introduced as part of a NATO programme to make aircraft and buildings less conspicuous from the air* (BAC).

Left *A No 19 Squadron F 2A at readiness in its QRA shelter at Gütersloh* (Peter March).

Below left *A No 92 Squadron F 2A is scrambled from its QRA shelter in Germany. The proximity of the refuelling probe to the access ladder, shows how easy the involuntary gymnastics described in the chapter on flying the Lightning, can be* (MoD).

Below *The camera aircraft moves in really close to a pair of F 2As of No 92 Squadron airborne from Gütersloh* (RAF Germany).

Above *A Lightning F 2A of No 92 Squadron formates with a Harrier of No 4 Squadron over Germany. At this time (January 1977) No 92 was the sole RAF Squadron operating Lightnings in Germany; the Lightnings were replaced by Phantoms later in the year (MoD).*

Left *An F 2A, XN771, of 19 Squadron and a T 4 in the drab green camouflage of the mid-1970s. The roundels and fin flashes are practically invisible (R.L. Ward).*

Below *This F 2A of No 92 Squadron shows its similarity to the F 6 as it enters a turn over German countryside during 1977. The aircraft has low-visibility markings except on the underside of the port wing (MoD).*

This particular squadron had suffered from low flying hours during July, due to constant fuel-leaking problems, and then until January 1968 had encountered horrendous problems in obtaining components such as tailplanes, trimmer switches, maxaret units, canopy parts and reheat fuel-pipes. One aircraft was grounded for 5 months awaiting a reheat fuel-pipe and another 76 days for a new jet-pipe. This frustrating situation resulted in the commanding officer eventually recording his thoughts in the following terms, which leave no doubt as to where the problem lay: 'The spares situation is a disgrace. Those responsible for the inept provisioning arrangements for the Lightning bear a grave responsibility. The tremendous efforts of the ground crews are invariably needed because of the shortcomings of the provisioning system.' It is difficult to find acceptable excuses for such a situation being allowed to occur on a front-line fighter unit, especially when it is remembered that at that time, the Lightning was the first line of defence for the UK and eight front-line squadrons were equipped with it. Budgeting for spares with a new aircraft is always difficult and at the end of the ten years from the infamous Sandys' White Paper, financial levels were still not back at the levels they would have reached if the cuts perpetrated by that paper had not been made. It must also be remembered that production of the Lightning was not intended to reach the levels of, say, the Meteor and Hunter, and components therefore followed a similar trend. But one of the most worrying aspects seems to be that some three years after the problems in the UK, the two German-based squadrons were still facing difficulties.

In September 1971, the spares situation on 92 Squadron had reached a critical level and was only eased in the latter half of the month by the use of components from Cat 3 aircraft awaiting repair — shades of the World War 2 hangar queens. Reheat pipes seemed to be the major problem with eleven being awaited by mid-October. By December 1971, the serviceability rate had fallen to 53.8 per cent, then it declined to 51.2 per cent by March 1972 rose to 71 per cent during April and in May plummetted to 48.5 per cent which meant that at this time less than half the Lightnings designated for interception work in vital German airspace were available to the squadron. Pressure from the unit's commanding officer and the technical officer saw a gradual improvement but, despite this, some typical delays in June 1972 were 15 days for a starboard tailplane, 7 days for a spring and 5 days for a trimmer switch.

Fortunately the problems gradually eased, and it speaks volumes for the servicing crews that the overall efficiency of the squadrons was not impaired, it was just a case of having to make do with fewer top-rate aircraft, a problem not entirely unfamiliar to the RAF. Taken in an overall context the serviceability on all the Lightning units was very high; the transient problems with spares obviously did not help and added an unnecessary worry to commanding officers but it is only right that they should be mentioned since it serves to underline the fact that, on an operational unit, life is not always as clear-cut as some 'official' statements indicate. To put the whole situation into perspective, it is perhaps sufficient to record that during the time the two squadrons in Germany occupied one of the west's most forward bases, their operational targets were always met and in many cases exceeded, on occasions 500 sorties per month not being unusual.

The F 2, with which both Nos 19 and 92 started their association with the Lightning, was the last of the first generation and the third single-seat variant to enter RAF service, though not the third type, as this was the T 4, which followed the F 1 and F 1A into service.

It had been evident from an early stage of Lightning development that a two-seat trainer version would be required. Thus, when the F 1 entered service, the method of converting pilots from the Hunter was far from satisfactory and it came as a great relief to many when the first two-seat aircraft, *XM970*, which had made its maiden flight on May 5 1961, was

Above *An F 3 of the 'Shadow Squadron' 2T which was part of 226 OCU* (Peter March).

Below *A T 5, T 4 and F 1A of 65 Squadron/226 OCU. The T 5 is armed with Red Top and the other two with Firestreak* (MoD).

Above *A Firestreak-armed T 4 of 226 OCU carrying the markings of the 'shadow' squadron, No 65. It was photographed at the Tiger Meet, Upper Heyford, on June 18 1971 where it was being flown by No 74 Squadron pilots* (R. L. Ward).

delivered to the Lightning Conversion Squadron (LCS) by Jimmy Dell and Sqn Ldr Robertson, on November 2 1961, being taken on charge by that unit on June 27 the following year. The LCS was based at Middleton St George, which had been the subject of an expensive update during the 1957–58 period and which was never to repay the taxpayers' investment, as far as RAF use was concerned, for in 1964 it was vacated when the LCS, which by then had become No 226 Operational Conversion Unit (OCU), moved to Coltishall and the airfield was sold for £340,000 to the local authority and became a civil airport serving the North-East.

The initial strength of the OCU was ten aircraft but these were later supplemented by F 1As, of which the T 4 was the two-seat derivative, and as a back-up to its primary training function the unit assumed the identity of No 145 Squadron for operational purposes. The T 4 was used to provide the necessary dual training for young pilots coming straight from the FTS, and they could expect to complete approximately 60 hours on the aircraft before going to a Lightning squadron, where they would spend several months before being declared operational. In the shadow role of an operational squadron, the instructors at the OCU flew both the T 4s and F 1As in Fighter Command exercises, to enable them to maintain their combat efficiency.

The T 4 was followed by the T 5 which was the two-seat version of the F 3, the first example, *XS419*, arriving at Coltishall on April 20 1965. Both T 4s and T 5s were also issued to operational squadrons where they were used for continuation training and practising instrument flying. Both two-seaters had full operational equipment and could therefore be used in all roles that the squadron's single-seaters were called upon to carry out. Most of the T 5s were distributed to the OCU and squadrons operating the F 3 where, in some cases, they replaced Hunter T 7s that had been fitted with Lightning instrumentation, which had performed notably as understudies pending the arrival of the two-place Lightning. One pilot, who had good cause to remember his first Lightning solo, was Flying Officer Fish, who was on the OCU course at Coltishall in 1966.

On July 1 he was flying T 5 *XS453*, on his first solo, when smoke filled the cockpit, he

Top *This T 5 of 226 OCU has twice suffered Cat 3 damage during its career, which commenced on December 18 1964, and continues until now where it serves as DW of the Lightning Training Flight at Binbrook* (MoD).

Above *An F 3 of 2T Squadron of No 226 OCU. The fin badge consists of the Latin 'II' superimposed on script 'T'. Note the spirals painted on the missile noses* (Peter March).

declared an emergency and attempted to lower the undercarriage before turning back to base. The gear failed to lower and the smoke persisted, so the pilot ejected safely five miles off the Norfolk coast. This T 5 which had made its first flight in the hands of 'Bee' Beamont almost exactly a year earlier (July 6 1965) had flown only 30.5 hours when it came to this untimely end. This particular aircraft and *XS460*, which incidentally had an even shorter life of just about 15 hours, were replaced by two new T 5s, *XV328* and *XV329*, which were built nearly a year after production of the aircraft had officially ended.

In May 1971, the initial-training squadron of the OCU took over the mantle of No 65 Squadron, as well as their T 4s, and F 1As soon began to wear the units' red chevrons on a white background marking; their role was unchanged, student pilots now being taught basic handling techniques before passing on to the T 5s of the advanced-training squadron. The latter also undertook the responsibility of training weapons' instructors, who were already experienced Lightning pilots.

The fourth single-seat Lightning to enter squadron service was the greatly improved F 3, though development of this did not move as quickly as had been hoped and consequently it was not released to the RAF until January 1964, when *XP695* was delivered to the AFDS at Binbrook on the first day of the month. Fourteen days later *XP696* also arrived at Binbrook and the final two F 3s of the AFDS' complement of four aircraft, *XP749* and *750* arrived in March and April. By February 1966, when the AFDS (as mentioned earlier) was renamed Fighter Command Trials Unit, only two of the F 3s remained and these departed soon after.

Above *A line-up of No 74 Squadron's F 1s. The picture was taken in 1961, when the unit was working up to becoming fully operational with the type* (BAC).

No 74 Squadron who were now located at Leuchars in Scotland, received their first F 3 in April 1964 when *XP700*, which had made its maiden flight on June 6 the previous year, arrived. This aircraft was assigned the code 'A' and became the commanding officers' mount; it was eventually passed to 29 Squadron in 1972 and crashed on August 7 of that year, after a take-off accident from Wattisham which caused Flt Lt Fenton to eject without injury. After June 1964, the squadron was able to say goodbye to its faithful F 1s, the last flight with this version being carried out by the squadron during July. No 74 shared Leuchars with No 23 who were to become the second users of the F 3 when they converted from their all-weather Javelin FAW 9s. In fact this was virtually a new squadron since most of the personnel were taken from other Lightning squadrons. No 23's first two Lightnings were *XP707* and *708* which arrived on August 19 1964. On August 28, Leuchars was stunned by a tragedy when Flt Lt Owen of 74 Sqd was killed while practising aerobatics for the forthcoming Battle of Britain Day. His aircraft was *XP704* 'H' and had only 36 hours 40 minutes flying time to its credit at the time of the accident. Events such as this naturally cast a gloom not only over the station but all personnel, and this one was particularly difficult as a large contingent of squadron personnel and relatives had been watching the rehearsal. However, both squadrons carried on with the task at hand, and in early 1965 were declared operational on the F 3.

Flight refuelling naturally featured highly in the training schedule as the latest Lightnings were still lacking in useful endurance. Much of the early practice was carried out in conjunction with USAF KC-135s as in 1964 fatigue cracks had been discovered in the Valiant, leading them to be withdrawn from RAF service, and the proposed replacement Victor tankers would not be ready for service until 1965. When the Victors began to operate from their base at Marham, it soon became normal for them to be detached to points along a planned Lightning route, in the case of an overseas deployment, or to rendezvous points in patrol areas when the fighters were being called

Above *A 56 Squadron F 3, this aircraft also served as 'G' with Nos 74 and 29 Squadrons. It was with the MoD on contract work with BAC at Warton in 1981* (Peter March).

Above right *A Red Top-armed F 3 of No 111 Squadron makes a low-level pass over HMS* Blake *some 70 miles off the coast of Malta. Note the squadron badge above the port missile* (MoD).

Right *A pleasing, port side view of a No 111 Squadron F 3 armed with Firestreak missiles. The marking above the No 111 badge on the fin is in fact a miniature of a No 56 Squadron's Phoenix* (MoD).

Bottom right *A 'Treble One' Squadron F 3 on its final approach into RAF Finningley in September 1974* (Roger Lindsay).

upon to investigate intrusions into UK airspace. The latter was becoming much more frequent during 1965, with Soviet reconnaissance aircraft attempting to gather electronic intelligence, as well as testing defences, in areas to the north of Scotland. The Lightnings aimed to intercept the hostile aircraft some 250 miles off the coast and needed the Victor tankers to replenish them while they shadowed the intruders.

The two Wattisham-based squadrons, Nos 56 and 111, were the next to convert to the F 3, receiving their first examples in February 1965 and December 1964 respectively.

At this time most Lightnings were finished in a natural aluminium and there was great rivalry among the squadrons to outdo each other with flamboyant markings. In 1965, No 56 painted the fins of their F 3s with red and white checkers, and the squadron's Phoenix badge appeared in a white disc surrounded by an arrowhead, forward of the fuselage roundel. The markings, and those adopted by the other Lightning squadrons, certainly equalled anything the American Navy could muster on their gull-grey F 4s and A 4s, which were renowned throughout the world for their imagination and colour. Such markings only lasted until the end of 1965, by which time officialdom put a stop to them, restricting squadrons to unit markings either side of the nose roundel and a squadron badge on the fin. Occasionally aircraft did appear with more adventurous markings, but they never reached the peak they had done in 1965 in the heyday of the F 3.

Treble One formed a twelve-aircraft aerobatic team during the spring of 1965, eleven of the aircraft being F 3s and the other the squadron's T 5. Performances at air displays throughout the country were always popular and spectacular, with numerous tight turns, plenty of reheat and a good leavening of rolls and loops being the usual ingredients. But no show was as spectacular as that on June 26 1965 at Exeter, when Flt Lt Doyle, flying F 3 *XR712*, gave his usual polished solo performance, which he concluded with a high-speed (Mach 0.92) run, only to have No 1 engine catch fire and his aircraft start to drop large parts of its tailpipe over the airfield. He headed back to St Mawgan, which was his base for the display, but had to eject before he could land, and a No 22 Squadron Wessex recovered Flt Lt Doyle from the sea; fortunately his only injury was bruising to his back.

Two months later Flt Lt H. Molland also had to make a descent, courtesy of Martin-Baker, when both engines of his F 3, *XP739*, flamed out five miles from the end of the Wattisham runway. The pilot was not injured and landed safely at Chapel Farm, Stoniham, whilst the aircraft, which had nearly 177 flying hours to its credit, ended its days at Battisford.

In September 1965, one of No 56 Squadron's F 3 aircraft, *XP765*, was displayed at Cranwell with dummy long-range tanks fitted above the wings, these being a foretaste of what was to come with the F 6. But the definitive version of the Lightning was still some way from squadron service and, in October 1966, No 56 took its F 3s, without the dummy tanks, to Malta for ADEX 66, where it acquitted itself with honours. The results of the exercise indicated that the Lightning was a first-rate interceptor, a point that had never been in doubt with any squadron. However, it had provided 56 Squadron with some sobering examples of the limits to its effectiveness the previous December.

At that time, which was in fact just a month after General Amer Khammash, the Chief of Staff of the Royal Jordanian Air Force, and six of his staff had visited Wattisham to have the Lightning demonstrated to them, the squadron had been involved in missile interception exercises in which the 'hostile' aircraft had been Hunters. The final analysis showed that, providing the Lightning had the element of surprise, it could be manoeuvered into position to fire its missiles, but with good Ground Control Interception assistance, the Hunter had a fair chance of survival, the Lightning kill rate being only 20 per cent.

With 1965 ending on this rather depressing note, No 56 had a disastrous start to the new year, when Flying Officer Derek Law was killed in a most sad and tragic way. On January 5, after being airborne for about 20 minutes the pilot of *XR721* reported that his radar was unserviceable and that he was returning to base, to carry out instrument approaches. After completing a GCA, he asked for a practice crash diversion to nearby Bentwaters. Seven miles from the end of the runway his number 1 engine flamed out and he declared an emergency, two minutes later he announced that he was unable to maintain height and was going to eject. Nothing further was heard and the aircraft crashed eleven miles east of Wattisham. It seems that after attempting to eject, the canopy failed to leave the aircraft, and the pilot was therefore forced into a dead-stick landing, a particularly difficult task in an aircraft like the Lightning. The landing was accomplished with a great deal of success, the underside of the machine suffering comparatively little damage, but just before it came to rest it struck a small fence, the canopy detached itself and the seat, which had been activated, went off and killed the unfortunate pilot.

The death of any member of a squadron is of course felt very keenly, but in cases such as this where the man concerned had displayed a very high standard of skill in a situation that escalated beyond his direct control, it is doubly difficult to bear. However, by the end of the year, 56 was back to its best and, in April 1967, the unit departed to Akrotiri in Cyprus to take over responsibility for the air defence of the island from the Javelins of No

29 Squadron, which now returned to the UK to be disbanded prior to being reformed on May 1 at Wattisham with F 3 Lightnings, most of which were ex-No 74 and 23 Squadron aircraft from Leuchars.

During the crisis in Cyprus in 1967, No 56 flew 50 battle scrambles in circumstances where the slightest error of judgement could have caused a major incident. The squadron operated its F 3s in Cyprus for four years, until it started to re-equip with F 6s which were from No 74 Squadron in Tengah, which flew the aircraft from Singapore to Cyprus when it was disbanded in August 1971.

Below XS928 *seen here at readiness with No 56 Squadron in Cyprus had a chequered career. It was first used by No 74 Squadron and was extensively damaged by fire at Tengah. After repair, it went to 23 Squadron at Leuchars and then to 56 in Cyprus. It is currently with No 11 Squadron at Binbrook, coded 'BJ', and was displayed at Abingdon's Battle of Britain Day in 1983, wearing three-tone grey camouflage (Peter March).*

The F 3 was built in greater quantity than any other version. Seventy were orginally ordered, some of which were modified to F 6 standard before delivery, and these were followed by a batch of 16 Interim F 3s *(XR752–XR767)* which were, to all intents and purposes, F 6s. The F 6, of which 39 were built *(XR768–773, XS893–904* and *XS918–938),* started to arrive with the RAF in November 1965 when *XR753,* one of the F 3 interim F 6s, was delivered to Binbrook's Fighter Command Trials Unit on the 16th.

Before that however, the dual-control version of the F 3, the T 5, was introduced into service with the arrival of *XS419* at 226 OCU Coltishall on April 20 1965. Like the T 4 the new two-seater had full operational capability and was regularly used in this capacity by the squadrons. Twenty-two T 5s were built and 21 of them were issued to the RAF, of which 15 were used by the OCU, although these were not all delivered initially to Coltishall. Twelve aircraft went direct to Coltishall and, later, some of them were allocated to squadrons, when in turn some squadron aircraft were transferred to the OCU. Some of the T 5s and a larger proportion of their single-seat counterparts, the F 3, still serve today with the LTF and Nos 5 and 11 Squadrons.

The first squadron to take delivery of the F 6 was No 5 which, until October 1965, had been flying Javelins in Germany. The squadron was disbanded on October 7 and reformed the following day at Binbrook, although it was to be nearly a month before it received its first Lightning, this being a T 5 which was delivered on November 19. Prior to this, No 5 had been operating a Hunter T 7 *(WV318),* one of eight such aircraft modified to have Lightning F 3/F 6 OR946 instrumentation, whose function was to serve as systems trainers until the T 5 Lightning arrived. On December 10, the first two F 6s arrived at Binbrook, these being *XR755* and *XR756,* followed soon after by *XR754.* It is of interest that these three aircraft were still at Binbrook in 1983, 18 years after their wheels first kissed the Lincolnshire airfield's runway.

Below *An F 3 of No 56 Squadron undergoing major servicing. The nose guard and tool-kit in the foreground in which every tool is identified by a silhouette, are of interest* (Peter March).

Above *A quartet of 56 Squadron F 3s over Cyprus during 1969. Note the variety of weaponry carried by the aircraft* (Peter March).

Lightning production never reached spectacular levels, and with an average of three aircraft a month leaving the factory, it took a little while to supply those squadrons converting or taking delivery of F 6s for the first time. It was not until March 8 1966 that No 5 Squadron's complement of twelve aircraft was completed with the delivery of *XR765*, another interim F 3/F 6. The rather slow delivery rate delayed the unit's work-up to operational status, which was also affected by some other, unusual, problems.

One of these was the apparent reluctance of certain aircraft to raise their noses on take-off, even when full back-pressure was applied to the control column. On June 16, Beamont visited Binbrook to look into this tricky situation which had been more than a little troublesome with *XR762* (K), an aircraft that had flown for the first time on October 9 1965 and had been delivered to No 5 Squadron on February 22 1966 by Captain Barr of the USAF. The BAC chief test pilot carried out tests on the aircraft, after which the nose wheel oleo pressure was increased to ensure that it did not have a nose-down attitude during the take-off run, this simple expedient quickly solving the problem and giving the squadron one less worry. During February 1967, some of the pilots of No 5 were presented with a unique opportunity to fly what had been one of the Lightning's rivals to equip NATO air forces.

A Dutch air force squadron, flying F-104s, visited Binbrook, on one of the regular exchanges that were commonplace during the sixties and seventies. The Dutch pilots were flown in the unit's T 5 and were unanimous in their praise of the aircraft, whereas the British pilots found many shortcomings in the F-104 and were not at all impressed by it. This rather innocent exchange goes a long way to supporting the long-held belief in aviation circles that, given the right backing from the government of the time, the Lightning could well have been bought by West Germany instead of the F-104, and such a purchase could have lead to its adoption by other NATO countries.

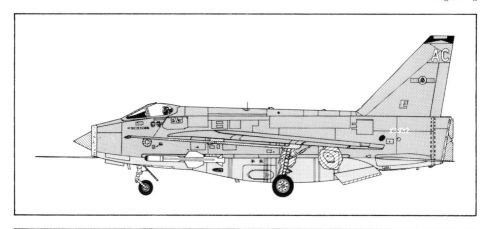

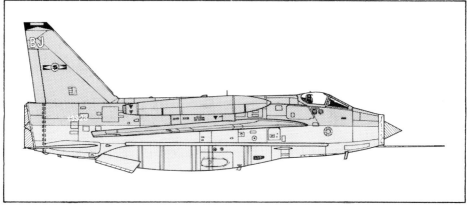

Top *Lightning F 6 XS932 'AC', No 5(F) Squadron, RAF Binbrook, 1983. Upper surfaces of fuselage, wings, tailplanes and fin in semi-matt dark sea grey; undersides of fuselage in semi-matt medium sea grey; undersides of wings and tailplanes, and refuelling probe, in semi-matt Barley grey (BS4800.18B.21).*

Above *Lightning F 6 XS928 'BJ' No 11 (F) Squadron, RAF Binbrook, 1983. Finish as for F6 of No 5 Squadron, except that demarcation line between upper-fuselage dark sea grey and lower-fuselage medium sea grey is set higher.*

The F-104 had the ability to get to Mach 2 very quickly, but had severe limitations in other directions. Lockheed had laid down a big production line for the aircraft, but the USAF cut its requirements quite dramatically when it was realised that the aircraft did not fulfil the operational parameters that they had specified. At this time (1958) Europe was looking for a supersonic fighter and, as the Americans had surplus production capacity for the F-104 they pushed their sales campaign into top gear in a market that was ripe for the picking. It was realised that if West Germany selected the American fighter, there was a very good chance that, in the interests of standardisation, most NATO countries would follow their lead.

An aggressive, but polished, American sales campaign which offered the opportunity for licensed production in Germany and Holland, as well as training in the USA, quickly established a foothold that it was impossible for the British to match. Beamont who had

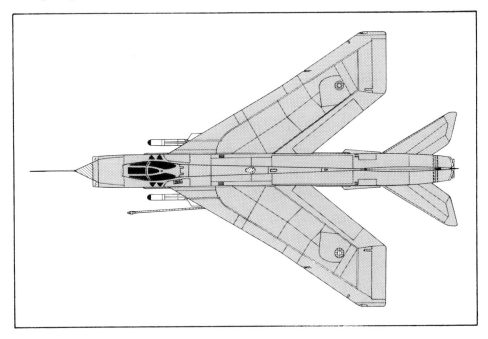

Above *Lightning F 6 — typical upper-surface plan view for Nos 5 and 11 Squadron machines in finish described.*

Below *Lightning F 6—typical under-surface plan view for Nos 5 and 11 Squadron machines in finish described; note 'dummy' canopy under nose, in natural metal. Upper-surface, dark sea grey returns onto underside leading edges of wings and tailplanes.*

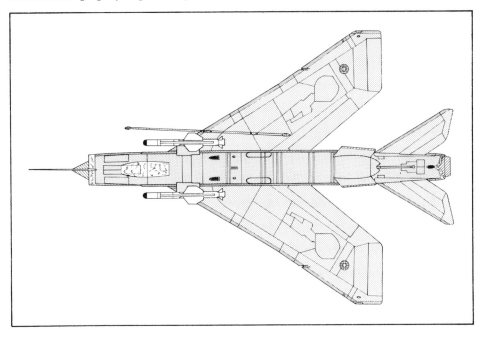

flown the F-104 was well aware of its limitations and knew that the Lightning was a much superior all-round machine. But the government had already indicated that money for future development of the aircraft was likely to be in short supply and its limiting fuel capacity seemed, at the time in question, a problem that would not be overcome.

A situation had also arisen whereby the British Government hoped to sell the Saunders-Roe rocket-powered fighter, a machine the RAF had already indicated that it did not want, to the West Germans. The latter was therefore very much favoured and given support that was denied the Lightning team, who were fighting against odds stacked against them by their own government who had made it patently obvious in Bonn that the English Electric aircraft was not in their view suitable for West German needs. If the aircraft had not been hampered by bureaucracy it is possible that the essential requirement for longer range would have been resolved much quicker, and as many as 500–600 aircraft could have been seen wearing the markings of NATO air forces.

However, this was all well in the past in 1966 when the F 6, with its greatly increased fuel capacity began to make its impact felt with the squadrons. No 74 started to exchange their F 3s when they began to receive the new aircraft in August 1966. This was the first

Below *A Red Top-armed F 6 of No 5 Squadron in natural aluminium finish. This aircraft was still with the Squadron at Binbrook in April 1983 when it carried the code 'AK' (MoD).*

squadron to receive full production-standard aircraft, the first being *XR768* which arrived in the hands of Flt Lt McEwan on August 1. This particular F 6 had a long life with No 74 and No 5 Squadrons, accumulating 2120 hours flying time before crashing into the sea off Mablethorpe on October 29 1974, when the pilot, Flt Lt Jones, who ejected safely, could not relight the engines after a double flame-out. During the build-up period No 74 flew F 3s and F 6s but, by December 1966, all twelve of their allocated aircraft had arrived at Leuchars. The concern relating to on-board fuel loads for the F 1, and F 3 previously operated by No 74, and their relief at the improved situation with the arrival of the F 6, is shown by an entry in the squadron's diary for October 1966, which states, 'The two Mk 6s started flying this month and having converted most of the pilots, we commenced finding new methods of burning up all that fuel!!'

During January 1967, the squadron became involved in flying five-hour flghts around the UK, cruising at 35,000 feet and only descending to refuel from Victors. This was the prelude both to a planned overseas deployment, in the Far East, and to a trip to Cyprus by four F 6s, in which they used over-wing tanks, that was carried out at the end of the month and proved that longer trips were easily within reach.

During March, two additional trials were set up for the squadron. The first of these involved an arrestor hook system devised by BAC and the second the investigation of compatibility of the F 6 with over-wing tanks with the Victor tankers.

In the first trials, a spring-loaded arrestor hook was fitted to the rear fuselage of the aircraft, this being released by the pilot to engage a wire stretched across the runway 400 yd from the upwind end. The official name for this gear was the Rotary Hydraulic Arrestor Gear, but it quickly became christened the 'Water Twister' because of the principal on which it operated. Trials were totally successful and all Lightning F 6s and F 2As were fitted with the equipment. The refuelling trials required a minimum of two receiver sorties to establish the flight-refuelling envelope, and a further 24 on cross-country routes.

The first sortie was flown on March 10 and the last on March 31 and, during this period, the target of 26 was exceeded by one, the tests absorbing 96 hours of flying time. Serviceability was good, the tanks giving no trouble apart from two cases of fuel venting from the base of the pylons. Two minor accidents occurred during the trials, the first being when the cross-wind component reached the limit for an aircraft with over-wing tanks, causing one Lightning to burst both main tyres and leave the runway. The second was when the fuel-dump switch was operated in mistake for the ventral tank's emergency-transfer switch. Both aircraft suffered only superficial damage and were soon back on strength, having played an important part in what was to be the longest ever 'hop' undertaken by single-seat fighters to take-up an overseas development.

The scene was now set for Exercise Hydraulic — the transfer of No 74 Squadron from Leuchars to Tengah on Singapore island. But before this another notable event took place, this being the first live firing of the Red Top missile by a squadron pilot. On April 12, Flying Officer P.A. Frieze became the first operational pilot to successfully fire a Red Top from a Lightning. The missile had performed disappointingly in its trials and there was little faith in its capability among those who were to use it as an operational weapon. Although the Flying Officer's launch was carried out in texbook style at low level, and the missile left the aircraft cleanly, it soon entered a series of violent convolutions during which it shed all its control surfaces before plunging to a watery grave. Confidence in the weapon took a further knock when Flt Lt P.M. Jewell fired another which exploded in spectacular fashion soon after leaving the aircraft. The cost of carrying out live firing trials with the Red Top was very high, but it was essential to have a weapon which could be relied upon, and at this time most Lightning pilots wished they had cannons to

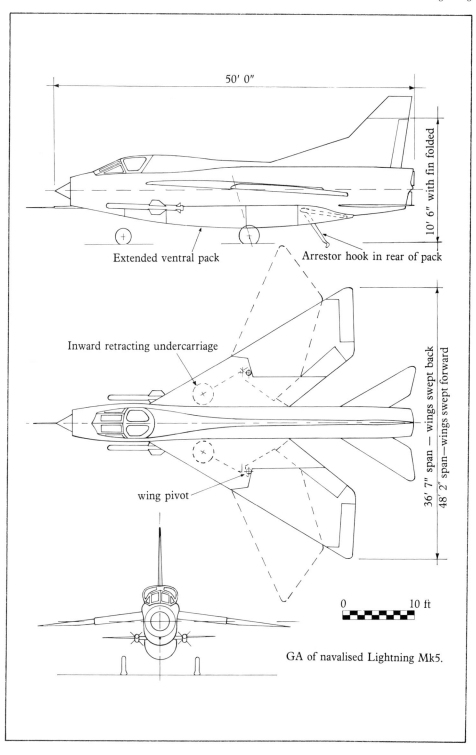

50' 0"

10' 6" with fin folded

Extended ventral pack

Arrestor hook in rear of pack

Inward retracting undercarriage

wing pivot

36' 7" span — wings swept back

48' 2" span—wings swept forward

0　　　　　　10 ft

GA of navalised Lightning Mk5.

Above *This No 11 Squadron F 6 eventually went to No 74 Squadron and was destroyed on July 27 1970 when it crashed on take-off from Tengah. It fell into a Malayan village, destroyed over 100 dwellings, injured two villagers, and killed its pilot Flight Lieutenant Whitehouse* (MoD).

supplement their suspect missile armament, the OCU's F 1As being the only Lightnings thus equipped at that time. However, on June 1 the trials and tribulations of faulty missiles and continual practicing of in-flight refuelling were put behind, when the advanced party left for Singapore.

With the ground-support parties established at the staging posts, it became the turn of the Lightnings to leave Scotland, which they commenced to do on June 4 when six aircraft led by Wing Commander Ken Goodwin took-off and headed for Cyprus. The following day, five more Lightnings departed and, on June 6, the last two single-seaters completed the evacuation of 74 Squadron from the UK. The aircraft were refuelled by a total of seventeen Victors of Nos 55, 57 and 214 Squadrons, and staged through Cyprus, the Persian Gulf and the diminutive island of Gan in the Indian Ocean. All thirteen Lightings had arrived in Tengah by June 11 and were fully operational the following day. The squadron's T 5, *XS416* (T) was handed to No 11 Squadron as it lacked the fuel capacity of the F 6s, and would therefore have required more refuellings, which would have added an unacceptable dimension to the route planning. The aircraft was replaced by *XV329* which was delivered to Short Brothers in Belfast on March 3 to be prepared for sea shipment to Singapore, a journey during which it suffered from salt corrosion to its starboard tailplane and No 1 hatch. On arrival at Tengah the aircraft was repaired, coded 'T' and delivered to the squadron, thus bringing the total strength to 14 aircraft. During the next four years, No 74 was the only air-defence squadron in the Far East Air Force, and made a vital contribution to the RAF's capability in this area.

The weather in the Far East was a great contrast to that left behind in Scotland, and soon both pilots and ground crews had settled into the new environment. Adjustment to the superb flying conditions did not take long and the Lightnings were fully occupied with practice scrambles and interceptions within a short time. Serviceability was also maintained at a high level despite some early problems created by crews getting used to local working conditions.

In January 1968, the friendly rivalry that has always existed between the RAF and Royal Navy continued, with an exercise involving No 74's Lightnings and Sea Vixens from HMS Eagle. The object of the exercise was for a pair of Sea Vixens to cross a line across Jason's Bay, without being intercepted by the RAF fighters. The RAF pilots were in for a shock if they thought that tackling a subsonic aircraft was going to be easy, since the Navy had worked out some tactics that were to produce some amazing results.

The Sea Vixens approached their task by splitting four aircraft into two pairs, one couple being designated Vixen 'bombers' and the other their fighter escort. The 'bombers' flew at 30,000 ft making use of cloud cover where it could be found, and the pair of fighters flew at 43,000 ft leaving a tell-tale con-trail. The result was that the interceptors could either be enticed towards the 'trailing' Sea Vixens, thus allowing the 'bombers' to sneak through, or they could detect the 'bombers' and attack them.

In the case of the latter option, the 'bombers' turned through 90°, thereby permitting the fighters to descend into the Lightnings in a quarter attack. This technique, if nothing else, proved that the sophistication of the Lightning's capability could be neutralised by the employment of imagination in the use of inferior equipment. On some occasions the Lightning's sheer advantage in speed proved to be an embarassment, an example being when the Ground Controlled Interceptor set up a head-on displacement of 20 miles through which the Lightnings would transit at Mach 1.3. By using wide-band homers, the Sea Vixens detected the Lightning's AI and were able to turn towards them and eliminate the vital displacement, at which point their high speed could become acutely embarrassing to the Lightning pilots. The end result of the exercise was that, out of the four attempts made by the Sea Vixens to cross the defined line, on one occasion the 'bombers' were successfully intercepted just prior to bomb release, but on the other three they achieved their objective, albeit with the loss of their escorting fighters.

It was exercises like this that enabled pilots to turn theory into practice and, where necessary, revise procedures which had been devised on what was thought to be well founded assumptions.

The following month another exercise was held, this time the enemy forces being represented by Mirages, Sabres, Canberras, Hunters and Meteors. The Mirages and Sabres belonged to the Royal Australian Air Force and operated from Butterworth, while the others were flown by RAF pilots from Tengah and Changi.

Attacks were made at all flight levels and, of 54 interceptions, it was officially estimated that 65 per cent were destroyed before weapons' release. The Lightnings flew 29 sorties and were credited with 13 confirmed kills, one of these being the only Mirage that was intercepted prior to releasing its weapon. With the lesson of the Sea Vixens' success still in mind, it is chastening to note that three Meteors flew in a straight line at 20,000 ft and were not intercepted, either inbound or outbound from their target. However, the Lightning pilots did prove that, in air combat with the delta-winged Mirage, their aircraft were superior and could out-manoeuvre the French machine, however well it was being handled by its Australian pilots.

But it was not all military exercises and there were many occasions when pilots used the ideal flying conditions to practice aerobatics, visual interceptions and the 101 other things that combine to make any fighter pilot total master of his machine and its systems.

In the middle of 1968, Lightning *XR770*, which was in fact the aircraft displayed in Saudi markings at the 1966 SBAC Farnborough air show, was fitted with a modification to the cockpit ventilation system. This was to enable air which was normally exhausted behind the seat, to be brought around the canopy frame to exhaust through variable-position louvres on either side of the pilot's head.

Sqn Ldr A.R. Fraser was attached to No 74 from the Ministry of Technology to supervise the tests, which were to be carried out on a simulated low-level sortie. Sensors were attached to the aircraft's cooling air-ducts and to the pilot, with readings being taken from these every five minutes. The trials were not an unqualified success, as many of the readings obtained could not be reconciled with the ambient temperature and, on some early flights, the Lightning's water cooler was found to be malfunctioning. It probably came as some light relief to the 74 Squadron pilots when, after the aircraft had been put right, it was tested again only for the pilot to discover that he suffered more from the heat than a pilot flying an unmodified machine!

In the early days of the Lightning's career with the RAF, permission had been given to carry out interception of the USAF's high-flying spy-plane the U2, a feat which the F 3s achieved without difficulty. In October 1968, No 74 reminded the USAF that the stratosphere was not entirely their own domain, when a pair of F 6s from Tengah, intercepted and carried out simulated attacks on a USAF RB57F, at an altitude at which the American crew had every reason to believe they were safe from manned interceptors.

During 1969, it was business as usual for No 74, the highlight of the year being a four-aircraft detachment to Darwin in Northern Australia in June 1969 to take part in Exercise Town House. The aircraft were refuelled 3 times during their flight to Darwin, spent seven days 'down under' and achieved a high kill rate in the exercise.

In August 1970, a major defence exercise involving land and air forces of five nations took place to test the defences of Singapore and Western Malaya. The Lightnings flew standing combat patrols supported by the Victor tankers of 214 Squadron and acquitted themselves well against intruding Canberras and Vulcans. Many of the interceptions took place at night and far out to sea, proving that the sobering lessons of the Sea Vixens and Meteors in 1968 had been well learned and digested.

August also saw a remarkably narrow escape by one of the squadron's pilots when he ejected from Lightning *XS893* east of Changi. Flying Officer M.D. Rigg, on returning to base, found that he was unable to lower his port main wheel and, as all efforts to release the recalcitrant undercarriage failed, he headed for the sea and ejected at 12,000 ft. This height was approximately 4,000 feet below the barometric capsule setting on the seat of 5,000 metres, consequently the main 'chute deployed instantly, the deceleration being sufficient to rip the stitching from the harness in the crutch loop. Although very severely bruised, Flying Officer Rigg managed to stay in the harness, his efforts subsequently

Below *A No 74 Squadron F 6, which was delivered on November 2 1966. The fin is all black and carries the squadron badge. This aircraft was still serving with No 11 Squadron at Binbrook in 1983, coded 'BD'* (Peter March).

causing much conjecture as to exactly how he had done this. After 30 minutes in the sea
the pilot was recovered by helicopter and taken to the military hospital. Following this
ejection — which incidentally had been witnessed by the squadron engineering officer
who was flying in a Shackleton at the time — the barometric setting on the Tengah-based
aircraft was quickly restored to 10,000 ft.

No 74 Squadron's tour of duty came to an end in August 1971 when British forces in
the Far East began to be run down. The Lightnings were flown to Akrotiri where most of
them were handed to No 56 and the 'Flying Tigers' were disbanded. During the period
that 74 were in Singapore, No 5 Squadron had replaced its interim F 6s with full-standard
aircraft and in 1968 undertook a non-stop flight from Binbrook to Bahrein, covering the
4,000 miles in eight hours and once again calling on Marham-based Victors to quench
their thirst en route. It fell to the squadron to mount a fly-past of six aircraft in July 1969
for the Investiture of Prince Charles at Caernarvon and in early 1970 they deployed to
Singapore to support 74 in local defence exercises as well as bringing back some of the
resident squadron's Lightnings for major overhauls.

No 5 Squadron who had won the Dacre Trophy for weapons' proficiency twice, were
honoured in May 1970 by the award of the Huddleston Trophy as the top NATO
interceptor squadron. This accolade came after two months of hard work, during which
they had competed with Mirages, F-102s and F-104s from eight other air forces in
Europe, during weather conditions that were to test their prowess as an all-weather
squadron. No 5 is one of the two squadrons still operating Lightnings from Binbrook
which it shares with No 11, the third unit to be equipped with the F 6, in April 1967.

No 11's history goes back to February 14 1915 when it was formed from part of No 7
Squadron at Netheravon. Among the personnel serving with the squadron in those far off
days was 2nd Lt G. Insall, who won the Victoria Cross while serving with No 11, and
Captain Albert Ball whose legendary exploits typify the period. Much of the squadron's
time has been spent abroad and after World War 2 it was formed into a night-fighter
squadron, initially with Mosquitos, then with Meteors and finally with Javelins, which it
was operating when it was disbanded in Germany in 1965. Reformed on April 1 1967, No
11 has operated the Lightning ever since and therefore shares with No 5 the honour of
being the longest-serving Lightning unit. In 1967, the prime task set No 11 was the role
vacated by No 74, that of the air defence of the UK, a task which it continues to have a

Below *A No 11 Squadron F 3 form Leuchars shows off its plan form at Greenham Common in 1976*
(R.L. Ward).

hand in from Binbrook, to which it moved in 1972.

In May 1967, No 23 Squadron also started to take delivery of interim F 6 Lightnings at Leuchars, but by the end of the year many of them had been replaced by full-standard aircraft, among which was *XS938*, the last Lightning to be produced for the RAF. This machine lasted until April 28 1971, when it crashed into the River Tay following a reheat fire, by which time it had flown just over 1233 hours. The pilot, Flying Officer McLean ejected safely. In 1968, No 23 Squadron flew two aircraft, *XR725* and *XS936*, non-stop across the North Atlantic to take part in the Canadian National Show in Toronto. The Lightnings left Leuchars on August 28 and returned on September 3 after performing several well received displays.

Increasing activity by the Soviet air force kept the two Leuchars-based squadrons on their toes throughout 1969 to 1972, these two squadrons receiving most of the interception work simply because of the routing of the Russian aircraft around the North of Scotland into the Atlantic. The occasional intruder which ventured down the East

Below *An F 3 of No 11 Squadron RAF Binbrook. Note the intake ring has been painted instead of being left in the more usual, natural-metal finish* (RAF Binbrook).

Bottom *An F 3 of No 11 Squadron shows the low-visibility markings to advantage. It is interesting to note that this aircraft is carrying no serial* (Peter March).

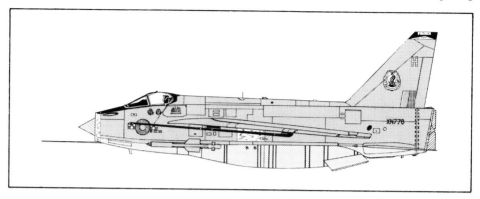

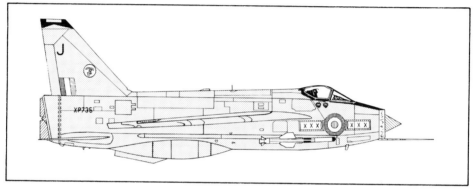

Top *Lightning F 2A XN778 'H', No 19(F) Squadron, RAF Gütersloh, Germany, 1974. Upper surfaces in semi-matt dark green, undersides in silver finish. Refuelling probe, matt black; Firestreak practice rounds in matt dark green.*
Above *Lightning F 3 XP735 'J', No 29(F) Squadron, RAF Wattisham, 1973. Overall finish as F 1.*

Coast was capably handled by Binbrook's Lightnings, which during this period maintained a 24-hour readiness on QRA.

The last RAF squadron to equip with the Lightning was No 29, which replaced No 56 at Wattisham, when the latter deployed to Cyprus in April 1967. At this time No 29 was at Akrotiri with its Javelin FAW 9s. Having handed over its responsibilities to the Lightning squadron, it returned to that unit's former base at Wattisham where it was reformed as a Lightning squadron on May 1. The first aircraft to arrive was a T 5, *XS422*, which arrived on May 10. This was followed by a complement of F 3s most of which had been previously operated by Nos 74 and 23 Squadrons. No 29 operated the F 3s until December 1974 when it converted to the Phantom. During 1972, the RAF had eight squadrons equipped with the Lightning and five of these had the prime responsibility of maintaining the integrity of UK airspace. Each squadron was split into two flights, one responsible for day flying and the other for night; the two-flight system works well and is still used by the two surviving Lightning squadrons.

In addition to the normal training role which included practice interceptions, scrambles, continuation flying, temporary overseas deployments and in-flight refuelling practices, every Lightning squadron was regularly involved in air-to-air missile practice, this usually being restricted to acquisition rounds, as financial restrictions placed a limit

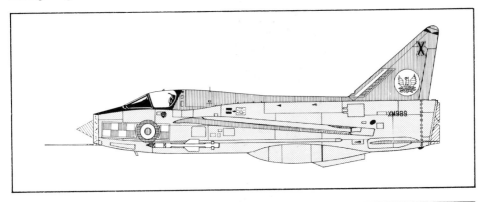

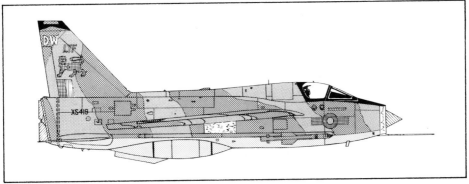

Top *Lightning T 4 XM989 'X', No 56(F) Squadron, RAF Wattisham, 1963. Overall finish as F 1, with gloss red dorsal spine, fin and rudder, and leading edges of wings and tailplanes.*
Above *Lightning T 5 XS419 'DW', Lightning Training Flight (LTF), RAF Binbrook, 1981. Upper surfaces in semi-matt dark green and dark sea grey, undersides silver.*

of five live rounds per squadron per year. Most of the live firing took place (and in fact still does) at RAF Valley where a Missile Practice Camp (MPC) is established. The tail-chasing Firestreak is used more often that not and its target is a heat source towed behind Jindivik pilotless drones.

In 1971, the RAF's Lightnings were progressively modified to carry the twin 30 mm Aden cannon-pack designed for the export F 53, this being fitted into the front part of the ventral tank. As previously mentioned, the missile armament is certainly limited in quantity and can present the pilot with problems in selection; the cannons therefore make the Lightning into a multi-armed interceptor, a situation that was and still is, very popular with pilots. One of the last major incidents in which the Lightning was involved came in July 1974 in Cyprus, when the coup staged by the Cyprus National Guard against President Makarios placed No 56 Squadron in the middle of a delicate situation.

During the period July 20-27 an emergency was declared and the Lightnings were brought to instant readiness, in a situation where increasing Turkish aerial activity was causing some concern. No 56 flew over 200 sorties, of which 110 were Battle Flights, 104 of these being executed during the period July 16-31. At the end of this very tense period, they had fulfilled their duties to the highest possible degree, had alleviated many potentially dangerous situations and had had no major problems with their aircraft. In

Above left *F 3 XP743 of No 29 Squadron shows off its Red Top missiles and flight-refuelling probe* (MoD).

Left *A No 56 Squadron F 6 touching down in Cyprus during a 1972 deployment* (Peter March).

Bottom left *The Phoenix badge and red and white chequer pattern of No 56 Squadron are very prominent on this view of* XS921, *landing from a sortie over the Med* (Peter March).

Above *Another 56 Squadron aircraft at readiness at Akrotiri during 1972.* XS929 *was one of the last F 6s to be built and was initially used by No 11 Squadron. It was in store at Binbrook, coded 'BC', during 1983* (Peter March).

fact, one difficulty that was thought might occur was the strain on pilots, but in the event this was not a major issue, although again on the lighter side, the squadron was happy to accept the services of Flt Lt Watson of No 11 Squadron who broke off his honeymoon in the island to help 56 spread the load!

At the time of the Cyprus crisis, Akrotiri was one of the RAF's biggest and busiest bases, but the defence review of 1975 reduced it to housing one squadron of search-and-rescue helicopters. This situation was short-lived because its potential as a base for an Armament Practice Camp (APC) soon became evident and in this capacity it is used extensively by current RAF aircraft including the Lightning. It is beyond the scope of this book to look too deeply into this facet of RAF operations, but it is necessary to take a brief look at the APC task in relation to the Lightning to conclude the story of the aircraft's RAF service.

Although target acquisition by radar and the use of air-to-air missiles is very much a part of the modern fighter, air-to-air gunnery using the original mark one eyeball to detect the target and conventional cannon armament to engage it in short-range, close-in combat, is still very much part of the fighter pilot's skill. Efficiency can only be achieved and maintained by regular firing with live ammunition, so all the operational squadrons in Europe have at least one session every year at an APC in Cyprus. It has been customary for the Lightning squadrons to spend five weeks in the Mediterranean, during which time the aim is to qualify their pilots for the NATO ACE (Allied Command Europe) qualification.

The Lightnings' route to Cyprus is via six in-flight refuelling rendezvous for the single-seaters and ten for the two-seaters, Victor tankers from Marham being the providers, with the ground crews being sent ahead of their charges. Although the T 5 is not armed, it is often taken to provide initial familiarisation with target interception for newer pilots, as

Above *The notice indicates that these F 6s of No 56 Squadron are fully armed. The second aircraft has the fins of its Red Top missiles painted with red borders* (Peter March).

well as giving some of the important, but often neglected, ground crews air experience. On occasions the gunless F 3 has also accompanied the F 6s, which, again, is used to provide air-interception experience and on some occasions to provide a practice interception target.

Each camp lasts approximately five weeks during which time the squadron pilots split into their two flights and alternate between operating their aircraft in a live-ammunition-firing role and the operations' side of the exercise. During the two weeks most pilots spend on the flying side of the deployment, they can expect to fly nine live-firing sorties, after getting the feel of things during a cine-camera work-up. The targets are banners towed on a 2,000 square-mile range by Canberras of No 100 Squadron, who usually fly two/three hour sorties, half-an-hour of which is taken in transitting to the range area. The Canberras fly a pattern dictated by the number of intercepting Lightnings, in the case of one aircraft it is a simple oval track, but with two interceptors a figure of eight is adopted. The 30 mm cannon is a lethal weapon, so naturally every precaution is taken to avoid a strike on the towing Canberra, which adopts a 30° angle of bank once the fighter has positioned itself. The interceptor must not come closer than 300 yards or a 12° angle-off, otherwise its mission is aborted. Every pilot flies cine missions until he has demonstrated that he can comply with the safety requirements; he is then cleared to fly six 'shoots' at the target with live ammunition to get his ACE qualification. This is a percentage score based on hits gained against rounds fired, the standard being laid down by SHAPE and common to all NATO air forces.

Gun movement, bullet spread and velocity jump, are some of the factors beyond the control of the pilot which have to be taken into account, as the combination of these can make the chances of hitting the target one in two for every round fired. It is therefore not easy to obtain good results but such factors as these are all taken into account in the scoring system adopted.

After completing the specified six sorties, the pilot then flies a limited sortie in which he is allowed a maximum of five passes at the banner. It is usual to start these with the familiar cine run followed by two live passes during which only 20 rounds per gun are used. In this exercise the Lightning meets the Canberra head-on, the tow aircraft then goes into a turn and both passes by the interceptor have to be concluded before 1½ cycles

Above *A 29 Squadron F 3 at Akrotiri during an Armament Practice Camp during 1974. The Squadron had operated Javelins from Cyprus and eventually exchanged their Lightnings for Phantoms* (MoD).

Below *A 57 Squadron Victor K1A refuelling two F 6s from Binbrook* (Peter March).

(540°) are completed. The banner is dropped over the airfield after each sortie and the scores carefully recorded, individual pilots' efforts being identified by coloured dyes applied to the ammunition. A competitive spirit is maintained throughout the year by the award of the Seed Trophy to the squadron displaying the most prowess in air-to-air gunnery during its APC detachment. The value of such annual deployments is consider-able and every year it serves to underline that although somewhat short-legged and still an awful lot of aeroplane for one man to handle, the Lightning gives a good account of itself and looks likely to be able to for a few years to come.

Background photograph *Two No 56 Squadron F 6s take a drink from a Victor tanker during a sortie from Akrotiri. The mountain is Mount Demavend, which at 18,392 ft is Iran's highest peak (MoD).*

Inset *Two No 5 Squadron F 6s demonstrate in-flight refuelling from a Victor Tanker from Marham (Peter March).*

Chapter 7

The Lightning in the 1980s

'With due respect to English Electric and the BAC, the aircraft is not exactly aerodynamically refined,* it has two bloody great engines, wrapped in an aluminium tube, an airframe that is exceedingly strong and a rate of climb that is still envied by many pilots flying more modern interceptors.' Thus spoke Wing Commander John Spencer, the commanding officer of No 11 Squadron, during a visit the author made to the home of the last two Lightning operational squadrons, RAF Binbrook, in October 1983.

Although it is now 25 years since the Lightning first entered RAF service, it still carries out a vital role in the defence of UK airspace and is likely to continue to do so until the mid-1980s. The two squadrons operating from Binbrook are Nos 5 and 11; they share the airfield with the Lightning Training Flight (LTF) which has the prime task of training Lightning pilots. All the Binbrook-based units operate T 5, F 3 and F 6 aircraft. Although now well into the twilight of a career that has gone well beyond the ten years forecast in 1958 and the planned mid-1970s phase-out, the Lightning is still a popular aircraft and, in the right hands and conditions, a formidable opponent.

Wing Commander Spencer, who has flown most versions of the Lightning and confirms the thoughts of many that the F 2A was the best of the breed, speaks enthusiastically of the aircraft that he and his fellow pilots now fly on a variety of tasks related to the policing of UK airspace. Both squadrons have a mix of new and very experienced pilots, some of the former coming to the Lightning straight from training on the Jet Provost and Hawk. Such pilots, who reach 5 or 11 Squadrons via the LTF, have a first and lasting impression of the aircraft's immense size, which is often followed by an equally lasting impression of its tremendous acceleration when they take it into the air for the first time. Pilots who have flown more modern fighters, still speak very highly of the Lightning, but stress that it is important to get comparisons into perspective. One pilot who had flown F 4s, F 15s and most versions of the Lightning, made the very valid point that although in many aspects of aerial combat the Lightning could hold its own against modern-day equivalents, it would, all other aspects being equal, usually be the underdog. Visibility from the cockpit is not as good as it might be and although it can accelerate faster than an F 4 and has an equal top speed, the workload on the pilot is very much higher.

In aircraft such as the Tornado and Phantom (F 4), there is a radar or weapons' system operator to interpret the interception radar, operate the ECM gear and generally place his aircraft in an attack position. In the Lightning this work is all part of the pilot's task; at the same time he has to concentrate on handling his machine, watching the fuel state and

*Author's note: the Wing Commander's comments must be taken in their correct perspective, since he is comparing modern designs with an airframe that is 25 years old, whose refinements were considerable at the time of its inception.

Above *An F 3 of the LTF at Binbrook returns to base after a sortie* (Andrew March).

Below *The ill-fated F 3 of the LTF, XP753, which won the Embassy solo jet aerobatic trophy at IAT 1983 and which was then lost with its pilot three weeks later in the sea off Scarborough* (IAT).

Above left and above *F 6*, XR726, *coded 'DF',*
of the Lightning Training Flight at the
International Air Tattoo, Greenham Common in
1983 (author's collection).

Left *An F 3 of Binbrook's Lightning Training*
Flight makes a low-level pass over a KC135 at
Greenham Common (Peter March).

Right *An LTF F 3 at Greenham Common for the*
1981 Air Tattoo (author).

ensuring that the correct weapons are selected. The latter can be quite tricky in a one-to-one situation, where the pilot is having to concentrate hard on what his adversary is doing, anticipate his next move and be ready to take evasive action or fire when in a position to do so. It could be that the Lightning is set-up for a missile attack, but circumstances change and cannons present a better option; in such a case the pilot has to virtually change hands to change the weapons selected and this can be a tricky task at high speed in a tight turn. The superb handling of the aircraft does of course help and is much commented on by the pilots. One of them told me, 'Unlike the F 4 the Lightning will warn the pilot if he tries to take too many liberties, or asks it to do something it doesn't like doing. If you ask it for too much it will give you a nudge, whereas the F 4 will simply refuse and perhaps leave you with egg on your face, or even worse.' A rather succinct way of summing up a big supersonic fighter that after 25 years front-line service is still very popular with air and ground crews alike.

Naturally the aeroplane must be flown and fought within its limits, and one of the latter is still what the crews rather quaintly term, 'its short legs', this referring to its short duration and range. In a full reheat climb, the Lightning consumes about 200 gallons of fuel a minute and though the rate drops to 10 per cent of that figure during a normal patrol, even so this only gives a combat duration of about 55 minutes, which is the average time for the day-to-day sorties flown out of Binbrook. The aircraft can of course be refuelled in flight and sometimes it is necessary to do this, when operational conditions require a Lightning to remain on station for long periods; on such occasions the limiting factor is pilot fatigue. The aircraft's cockpit is not exactly the most spacious in the world, and being trussed up in an anti-g suit, wearing survival gear and breathing oxygen continuously, does make demands on the pilot's concentration which, after a period of time, could obviously affect his fighting ability.

The main tasks of the two squadrons at Binbrook are, the defence of the UK in war, the policing of UK airspace in peace, the defence of the Royal Navy at sea and overseas deployment. The latter is not so frequent as it was a few years ago, but nonetheless there

Above, left and above *Two F 3s, one of the Lightning Training Flight and the other of No 11 Squadron, show their paces and their different missile installations* (Peter March).

Below *F 6 XR759 with over-wing tanks in three-tone grey camouflage at Honington in 1983* (R.L. Ward).

Above, below and opposite *A T 5 Lightning of No 11 Squadron undergoing servicing at Binbrook in October 1983. The engines have been removed and the myriad small panels contrast with present-day designs and their large removable sections* (author).

Above *F 6* XR783, *'AE', of No 5 Squadron on the flight-line at Binbrook on October 17 1983* (author).

Below *In 1983, Princess Alexandra visited the last three RAF units to be equipped with Lightnings, Nos 5 and 11 Squadrons and the LTF, at Binbrook. A fly-past of the unit's aircraft forming the letter 'A' was planned, but bad weather on the day prevented it taking place. This rare photograph taken during a rehearsal shows how precise the flying was* (RAF Binbrook).

Above *An F 6 of No 11 Squadron in grey/green camouflage contrasts with a similar machine in two-tone grey* (author).

Below *A No 11 Squadron F 6, XS923, on QRA at Binbrook* (RAF Binbrook).

Above *The grey and green camouflage on this F 3 of No 11 Squadron is still considered by many to be far more effective than the more recently introduced three-tone grey* (Peter March).

Opposite XR747 'BF' *of No 11 Squadron awaits its pilot on the Binbrook flight-line* (author).

are still exchange visits with NATO air forces in Europe.

The defence role is also changing, for whereas it was once confined mainly to antici-pated high-level penetration of UK airspace, there is now a growing requirement for low-level interception and this forms an important part of the Lightning squadrons' practice tasks. At low level the aircraft has an even shorter range and is perhaps not entirely suitable for this role, but it handles well, has a good weapons' system and will give an extremely good account of itself within the limits imposed by its greater consumption of fuel at low altitude. Carrying only two missiles the Lightning does suffer a disadvantage in this sphere but, time and again, it was pointed out that 30 mm cannons are extremely lethal and it was expected that in the conditions where the Lightning operates on equal terms, it would be a deadly opponent. Pilots who had studied combat reports from the Falklands pointed out that very short bursts of cannon fire had wreaked devastating damage to every type of enemy aircraft. They were also very soberly aware that such weapons would do their own aircraft no good if they were caught in the gun-sights of opponents, one pilot pointing out that in any modern fighter a hit almost anywhere is likely to lead to problems.

Practice interceptions usually involve two Lightnings flying in a pair, one protecting the other's tail. They operate together crossing over at the extremes of their defined patrol area, in such a way that one pilot is always aware of what is happening in the blind area of the other. The age-old tactic, used since the days of the 'string-and-paper' biplanes of World War 1, of using the sun and clouds, still very much applies as does the constant lesson of always watching your tail. In many intercepting situations the radar is switched off, as its emissions can be detected by the enemy aircraft's warning devices, but it is often used in a tactical situation where its sudden activation can cause an enemy to turn into a position anticipated by the Lightning pilot, who is then ready for the 'kill'.

Lightning pilots will always try to avoid high g turns, which can occupy a lot of

Above and above right XS933 *of No 11 Squadron is wearing the three-tone grey camouflage and low-visibility roundels, adopted in the early 1980s. It was photographed at Binbrook in October 1983* (author).

airspace, to bring them onto the tail of a potential enemy, since this can often result in a lengthy tail chase by which time the hostile aircraft could well have gained space in which to launch its offensive weapons. The ploy is to use the Lightning's assets, which are its ability to accelerate quickly and its climb rate; a quick climb and fast descent onto the enemy is much better than a turning combat, in other words, as the pilots like to say, 'we use the vertical plane and hope the enemy opts to turn and engage us, when that happens there is a good chance he is finished'. In less than ideal conditions; the aircraft is at a disadvantage mainly due to its avionics; there is no 'look-down' facility on the radar, which can leave an area through which an enemy can sneak, but this can be allowed for in a variety of tactical ways which were not discussed!

No 5 Squadron has been at Binbrook since 1965 and No 11 joined them there, from Leuchars, in 1972. No 5 was the first RAF squadron to be equipped with the F 6, which it received in 1965, and No 11 was the third squadron to operate the mark, receiving its first aircraft in 1967. So both units have nearly two decades of experience in flying the aircraft and their enthusiasm today is no less than it was when the aircraft was the service's latest interceptor. It is an infectious enthusiasm which almost seems to rub off on the very aircraft themselves, for although many of the airframes are now twenty years old, they still look part of a modern fighting force and their appearance almost seems to deny

one authority to write the final chapter of their long and distinguished service.

Sharing Binbrook with the two squadrons is the Lightning Training Flight which also operates the F 3, F 6 and T 5 marks, the latter being fully operational with dual controls and duplicated fire-control systems. It can therefore be operated in a two-man crew role, whereby one pilot flies the aircraft and the other concentrates on the weapons' systems — a method that reduces work load and therefore perhaps puts such a Lightning into the arena with a slight advantage over its single-seat cousin. When the Lightning OCU was disbanded in October 1975, the LTF was formed from 'C' flight of No 11 Squadron and it now has total responsibility for the training and conversion of all Lightning aircrew.

During the early 1980s, the Lightnings adopted a two-tone grey camouflage scheme and, during my visit to Binbrook in October 1983, some of the pilots commented that this camouflage made the aircraft stand out (sic) very well from almost any position and in all light conditions! Perhaps it is really just a ploy to keep the Lightning very much in focus, for although it is scheduled to bow out to the Tornado in the mid-1980s, it would not be too surprising if it was still carrying out vital tasks in the early '90s; it is certainly strong enough and has enough airframe life to be able to do so. If it does, there can be no doubt that there will still be pilots anxious to fly it and enthuse over its performance.

Chapter 8

Export Lightnings

Overseas sales of any high-performance aircraft are difficult, especially when there is competition in which political ambitions may well have more than a slight influence on the price finally offered to the potential purchaser.

The vast potential of the Lightning took a severe blow after publication of the infamous 1957 White Paper on defence. The belief that this was likely to be the RAF's last manned aircraft caused serious limitations in development. Money was always tight as far as the respective ministries were concerned, so the result was that in the first years of development the Lightning was strictly tied to its initial conception as a short-dash interceptor, which limited its immediate export potential.

The 1957 paper saw the cancellation of many promising British designs and it was not until the early 1960s that it became clear that the premise on which this was based was false. By that time, the British aircraft industry had been dealt a blow from which it never recovered; the future lay in amalgamations and multi-national consortia producing aircraft of questionable ability that sadly, in many cases, were far inferior to those that went under the 1957 axe, and in such actions as that of the Labour Government in the early 1960s, which cancelled such projects as the TSR2 and replaced them with imports from America.

As the Lightning became established with the RAF, the BAC began to look again at its export potential. Life was still difficult as far as development was concerned, but moves were already afoot not only to increase the aircraft's range — one of the initial limiting factors — but also its overall ability to perform roles other than that of straight interception. In 1963, the company received authorisation from the government to develop the range of the Lightning, primarily to assist in its deployment to overseas theatres. This gave the necessary impetus to looking once again at the whole situation regarding overseas sales, for it was already quite clear that the basic design was well capable of outperforming other aircraft then being toted around foreign market-places. If such authority had been given earlier, it seems very likely that the Lightning could well have equipped some of the NATO air forces, and its production could have run into two or three thousand airframes.

As it was, most European air forces were in the process of being equipped with American-designed aircraft, some of which were being built under licence in the countries purchasing them. The lucrative Middle Eastern market was wide open, and although the French Mirage was popular, there was still room for other contenders. Studies had been made by the BAC in relation to producing the Lightning for Austria, Japan, Germany, Singapore, Nicaragua and Brazil; in the latter case one aircraft was in fact made to their requirements.

Some of the studies were not without an element of humour as, for example, in the case of the Nicaraguan Lightning where it was discovered that there was nowhere the aircraft

Above *This F 3 was originally* XR722; *it carried the registration G-27-2 (later G27-2) before becoming 53-666. It was used on development flying for the Saudi contract and took part in SNEB rocket and bomb trials. It was delivered to Saudi Arabia on June 28 1969 and crashed on February 6 1972, the pilot, Captain Mohammad Saud, escaping successfully* (BAe).

could land and delivery by sea would have presented a problem on arrival, since the aircraft's wing-span was too wide to allow towing through the streets and the wings could not be detached due to the positioning of the undercarriage!

In the early 1960s, it was well known that the Saudi Arabian government were looking to strengthen their air force and had money to spend on a new defence system. In 1962, the Royal Saudi Air Force was a mere dozen years old and as well as being untried in a 'hot' situation was struggling with some fairly outdated equipment. In that year, fighting broke out on the Saudi–Yemen border, the dispute being largely ideological as the strongly royalist Saudi government gave its backing to the claimant to the throne in North Yemen, while revolutionary forces that had seized power on the death of Iman Ahmad were supported by President Nasser's Egyptian government. Russian-built IL-28 and MiG-17 aircraft, supplied by Egypt, intruded into Saudi airspace and there was little that the air force could do to stop them. This situation therefore led to the determination of the Saudis to acquire a completely new air-defence system.

When Crown Prince Faisal acceded to King Ibn Saud's throne, an agreement supporting a plebiscite in the Yemen was signed with Egypt. In the event, this did not occur and the intrusions, together with occasional bombing, continued to take place. Towns and settlements within a few miles of the Yemeni border were often the targets for strafing so the nearest Saudi airfield, which was located at Khamis Mushayt, became the centre for the strengthening of the Saudi defensive position in the south-east. Located

Above *Two T 54s for the Royal Saudi Arabian Air Force; these are equivalent to the RAF's T 4s* (BAe).

near the border with North Yemen which ran through mountainous country close to the Red Sea, it provided an ideal site for the deployment of interceptors, being only 54 miles from the nearest point on the Yemeni border.

Negotiations with Britain, intended to lead to the provision of a complete air-defence package, were started but an interim deal was arrived at whereby six Lightnings, six Hunters and a battery of Thunderbird SAMs would be supplied, in a package code-named 'Magic Carpet'. An English businessman, Geoffrey Edwards, played a key role in negotiating the hardware contracts as well as recruiting the necessary personnel, including pilots, air-traffic controllers and radar operators.

The six Lightnings covered by the Magic Carpet contract were all ex-RAF aircraft purchased back through the MUs where they were stored by the BAC. The company did in fact convert six F 2s which were re-designated F 52; the first of these was allocated the B-class civil marking *G27-239* and was in fact *XN734*, but though it was converted to full Saudi specification it was never dispatched to the Middle East.

The first four F 52s to be delivered to Dhahran, where they were received by Airwork personnel, were *XN796 52-657, XN770 52-656, XN767 52-655* and *XN797 52-658*; the latter three were later recoded *52-610, 52-609* and *52-611* respectively. *XN796* left England on July 8 1966 piloted by Tim Ferguson and was followed, three days later, by *XN770* flown by Don Knight. The other two aircraft departed together on July 22 1966, again in the hands of Knight and Ferguson. The two T 4s, which were reclassified as T 54s, were *XM992 54-651* (later *54-608*) and *XM989 54-650* (later *54-607*), these being

Above G27-57 *(ex G-AWOO) was the F 53 used for the flying display at the 1968 SBAC display, Farnborough. It is fitted here with Matra rocket pods under the wings. It became 53-687 and was delivered to Saudi Arabia on April 17 1969* (author).

delivered to Saudi Arabia by Ferguson and Knight on June 6 1966.

The Lightnings were immediately used to help restore public morale with several demonstrations including low-level beat-ups, formation flying and the ever popular full-reheat climb. The new might of the Saudi Air Force, which was replacing aged F 86s and World World 2-vintage B-26 Invaders, was usually demonstrated near the Saudi capital to obtain the best public-relations results. On one occasion, a pilot attempted to rotate too quickly after take-off to go into a full reheat climb, lost complete control of the aircraft and used his ejection seat to abandon the wallowing Lightning. This occurred on September 20 1966 at Riyadh and was the first serious casualty suffered by the Saudis with their new aircraft. The machine was replaced by *XN729 G27-1 52-659* (later *52-612*) which was delivered to Saudi Arabia by Peter Ginger on May 9 1967. Another F 52 was destroyed on November 28 1968 when Major S. Ghimlas was killed when attempting to carry out a single-engined landing but allowed his speed to decay too quickly and, with insufficient altitude, was unable to recover. As part of this original deal the Saudis also took delivery of several Hunter T 7s which were later passed to Jordan.

The Lightnings did not begin to arrive at the front-line airfield of Khamis until August 7 1967, when an F 52 and a T 54 arrived from Riyadh. Two more aircraft arrived on August 9, with the final two being delayed until the 18th due to strong cross-winds at their destination. Before the aircraft could be declared operational, adjustments to suit the airfield altitude had to be made to the AVPIN-fuelled starters, which proved to be a tricky

Above *Four unarmed F 53s in full Saudi markings await delivery* (BAe).

Left *A Royal Saudi Air Force F 53 about to touch down at Farnborough. The aircraft is carrying Matra rocket pods on the outboard wing pylons* (Peter March).

and lengthy task but by the 28th of the month it had been accomplished and two Lightnings celebrated their arrival in the front line by making several low-level passes across the airfield and around the local area.

The Lightnings were declared fully operational by November 13 and began regular stand-by duties. The arrival of the Hunters and Lightnings in the area clearly served its purpose because, from the moment they became operational, all attacks by Egyptian aircraft ceased, although there were the occasional intrusions, set up more for their nuisance value than for their strategic effect.

Although the presence of the Lightnings achieved its objective, many of the No 6 Squadron pilots were disappointed that they had never tested it in combat. The unit was often hamstrung by a lack of spares, fuel and the lack of any real sense of urgency in the RSAF control centre at Khamis where, on some occasions, the order to scramble a section of Lightnings was so delayed that the intruders were well back over the Yemen border before it came.

The eagerly awaited export order came to fruition in December 1965 when it was announced in the House of Commons that the British offer to Saudi Arabia had been accepted. The order subsequently received was one of the largest export contracts ever received by Britain and the defence package included 33 T 53s and six T 55s; the former figure eventually became 34 when an additional airframe was produced to replace one of the original aircraft which was lost in a crash.

The prototype F 53 was *XR 722*, which was one of the original F 3s earmarked for F 6 conversion. It carried the civil code *G27-2* and was dispatched to Saudi on June 28 1969 as *53-666*. Although designated F 53, the Saudi aircraft were not really derivatives of the F 3

Below *Three T 55s of the Royal Saudi Air Force. Note the large ventral tank which is the same as on the F 6. The RAF's T 5s all had the small ventral tank, and the RSAF T 55s were really derivatives of the F 53, which was basically an export equivalent of the F 6 (BAC).*

in the truest sense of the word, being more a development of the F 6 with provision for underwing pylons on which could be carried two 1,000 lb bombs or two packs of 18 SNEB 68 mm rockets. Additionally, it could also be fitted with a 48 2 in-rocket fuselage-pack and two 30 mm Adens in the front part of the ventral tank. The under-fuselage rocket-pack could also be replaced by a reconnaissance pack containing five Vinten cameras.

The modified F 3 made its maiden flight as an F 53 on November 1 1966 and was then involved in development work until its departure for Saudi Arabia. It reached No 2 Squadron at Khamis Mushayt on December 5 1969 and was lost on February 6 1972 when on loan to No 6, after Captain Mohammed Saud experienced an explosion in the gun bay.

An event which, only one year earlier, very few people would have thought possible had occurred, giving a considerable boost both to the British aircraft industry and to other industries associated with it. Many sceptics had dismissed the Lightning as a 'milk-bottle and razor blade' design, with no endurance, ferry range or ground attack capability, and so the announcement of the Saudi contract came as a shock to them and those who had written off the aircraft as another example of British short-sightedness. Having captured a market that at one stage was widely tipped as likely to go to the Mirage 111, the field appeared to be open for the BAC sales' team. But, sadly, events were overtaking them and although Kuwait eventually purchased 12 F 3s and two T 55s, Jordan, which was expected to follow suit, opted for the F 104 on loan from the USA and the Lebanon went for the Mirage 111. The announcement that the McDonnell Douglas F-4 Phantom would replace the Lightning in RAF service did not help the export campaign.

At that time the F 4 cost approximately the same as a Lightning, but with a two-man crew, newer radar, better range and heavier armament, it was considered to be more cost-effective than the two-engined single-seat British aircraft.

Saudi pilots were trained at 226 OCU before forming their own conversion unit in the Middle East. The last of the F 53s was delivered in August 1969 and, despite the original plan having been to form three squadrons, only No 2 became fully equipped with the aircraft, while No 6 operated a mixture of Lightnings and Hunters. Information on the present whereabouts or fates of the exported Lightnings is not officially available, but it is believed that many of them are in store, although what effect this may have had on the airframes and equipment is open to conjecture.

It is known that at least two of the Saudi F 53s were written off in accidents, and several more received up to Category 3 damage in ground incidents, but by 1971 the majority were still in service. Even less information is available on the 12 Kuwait F 53s, but again two were lost in flying accidents, one, *53-414 (G27-82)*, crashing into a shanty town on April 10 1971 killing 3 Arabs as well as its pilot. One other was written off in a ground accident and the rest are now being phased out of operational service and will presumably be placed in store.

The Saudi air force ordered the F 15 to replace the Lightnings and the Kuwaitis opted for the Mirage F 1; perhaps the lesson is that if the Lightning had been developed to its full potential from the very beginning and the British aircraft industry had not been ruined by the 1957 White Paper, and later political actions, there might well have been another, British, supersonic fighter serving in quantity in the Middle East.

Chapter 9

Flying the Lightning—a pilot's eye view

'One is conscious, when walking out to the aircraft, of just how big a machine it is for one pilot. The pre-flight walk-round confirms this view, especially for those of smaller stature — up on tiptoe to peer down the intake and walking under the wing without lowering one's head, perhaps to comment, "look at those narrow high-pressure tyres — no wonder they only last a few landings". The thin high-speed aerofoil wing dictated the use of a long spindly undercarriage with thin cross-section wheels and tyres. The 60° sweep-back of the wing means that the undercarriage legs have to describe an arc during retraction in order to lie along the wing line. If you stand under the wing and look where the wheel is supposed to go, it is hard to believe that the whole leg retracts so cleanly. One moves on round the tailplane, low set where the aerodynamicists said it shouldn't be and where it gives excellent longitudinal control. Make sure the braking parachute is stowed correctly under the lower jet-pipe with the cable securely in the clips around the pipes. Who ever thought of putting one engine atop the other? Now round the other side checking accumulator pressures and panels — especially the refuelling panel — for safety. At last, the ladder, surely one of the biggest cockpit-access ladders anywhere? Now comes the tricky bit — climbing up with all your flying kit on and squeezing past the refuelling probe. This 20-ft-long black "drain pipe", which is semi-permanently bolted on under the port wing, has given generations of Lightning pilots more than a few sore heads and has provided endless amusement for ground crews. Forget it is there when ascending and you bang your head — forget it when climbing down and the reverse [sic] happens. Many people have used the probe to swing down from the cockpit — which is fine until you forget there isn't a probe fitted! Even more embarrassing is to close up to the tanker and attempt to plug in a non-existent probe. Perhaps the best tale concerning probes is the one involving a certain Wing Commander who was OC [Officer Commanding] of an OCU [Operational Conversion Unit] squadron. The ladder on his aircraft was not properly secured but this did not become apparent until he was over half-way up and past the probe. The top of the ladder swung away from the aircraft and it looked as though he would fall 12 ft to the ground. Fortunately the probe caught him in the small of his back, his legs came up and he did a backward flip to land on his feet. He turned to the ground crew with great aplomb and said, "I do it every day for exercise". However, he returned to the crew room for a stiff coffee before attempting to fly again!

'Having got into the tiny but comfortable little "office", one arranges all the knobs and switches in a neat and eye-catching order, only using the shiny ones, (the rest are obviously not used) and attempt to start the mighty Avons. I say 'attempt' because this was always the exciting part of any sortie, the start. AVPIN — the starter fuel (Iso-propyl nitrate to give it the full name) is a mono-propellant fuel. Once ignited it needs no external air/oxygen to sustain combustion and thus is very unstable and highly volatile.

Above *The base of the refuelling probe and landing light of F 3 XR718 of 29 Squadron* (R.L. Ward).

Below and overleaf *The cockpit layout of the Lightning. Here the aircraft is a F 2A* (BAe).

Above *A 226 OCU T 5 departs from Lakenheath during a 1970 air display* (R. L. Ward).

The starters used to be somewhat temperamental and sometimes would fail to ignite. Hence the famous "whee-phut" noise which inevitably was heard on Lightning bases the world over. However, once one had engines running there was little else that could go wrong to prevent one getting airborne and so one can begin to taxi. Now if you can imagine driving a double-decker bus from the top floor you have some idea of taxying a Lightning. To steer the aircraft you push the rudder pedal and squeeze the brake grip on the control column. One can always tell a new pilot by the way the aircraft nods and bows its way along the taxi track. It takes a little while to get used to the subtleties of differential braking using hands and feet, especially in a raging cross-wind on a wet runway, so you know an experienced Lightning jockey by his well-controlled handshake.

'The pre-take-off vital actions [VA] the TAFFIO checks (the mnemonic is a hangover from piston days where it stood for Throttle (friction nut), Air (carb hot), Fuel, Flaps, Instruments and Oxygen), are gone through; the advent of jet flying extended the check list so that the Lightning VA actually reads TTAAAFFFIOHHH — it would need another chapter to explain them all.

'On the early "lightweight" Mk 1, 1A, 2 and 3 Lightnings, the normal take off was in cold (military) power. The Mk 2A, 6 and T5, being significantly heavier, required full reheat [R/H] take offs to provide an adequate safety margin should an engine fail during the take-off roll. The "rotation" take off, the eye-catching snap pull into a near vertical climb, was treated as very much a display item in latter years, although it used to be quite the norm in the mid-sixties. The technique was simple, and clearly showed the outstandingly predictable and straightforward handling characteristics of the aircraft. The nose was raised at around 140 kts and the aircraft lifted off at about 165 kts — it would not fly itself off, so a positive rearward movement of the stick was required. As the speed increased, one checked forward and aimed to level off at around 30 ft, trimming forward all the time to keep the stick force load free. At around 260–280 kts, a sharp rearward movement of the stick would give 2½–3 g, and rotate the nose through 60° or so. The speed would decay to 180–200 kts and one checked forward to fly a gentle bunted climb. Having now flown aircraft fitted with AOA indicators, I am glad the Lightning did not have one. I am sure the aircraft was "super-stalled" during the rotation but provided one kept rudder and aileron neutral, and 'captured' the climb altitude with a little forward

Above *A rather rare sight, nine F 6s of Nos 5 and 11 Squadrons airborne from Binbrook* (Peter March).
Above right and right *Two views of a camouflaged F 3 of No 11 Squadron at the Greenham Common Air Tattoo in 1976. The aircraft is* XR720 'M', *and in the lower picture it is just retracting its undercarriage prior to starting its display. The aircraft became 'DA' of the LTF in 1983* (Peter March).
Below right *Lightning F 3,* XR720, *arrives at Greenham Common where it took part in the 1983 Air Tattoo* (IAT).

stick, the manoeuvre was safe, clean and usually spectacular.

'Once airborne, even in cold power, the aircraft accelerated very quickly and one had to be quick to raise the nose at 430 kts to peg the climb speed at 450 kts. Similarly, it took concentration to ensure that one correctly converted to Mach 0.90 during the climb, otherwise it was easy to get supersonic in the ascent. The Lightning, although designed as a tropospheric interceptor, had an abundance of power throughout its flight envelope and this, coupled with the nicely balanced and harmonised controls, made the aircraft a natural for display flying. One could start from a rotation take off, although this often left one in a nose-high attitude at about 3,500–4,500 ft with little speed to manoeuvre. In addition, the need for 7000 ft of runway often meant that one displayed on a touring basis, that is, with a flying arrival and departure.

'So, let us "fly" through a typical display sequence from a flying arrival. "Lightning, you are clear for display", crackles through the headphones. Right — start the acceleration but leave the reheat until the airfield boundary. Ease down to 250 ft, trimming load free at 550 kt and lining up with the display axis. Note the altimeter reading and the surface wind — on-crowd winds are always a problem. Reheat in and wait for the light-up . . . both lit — good! Reef into a 90° bank turn, away from the crowd, to let them hear the roar of the burners and then cancel — airbrakes out to kill the speed and tighten the turn. Hold 6½ g until 420 kts, then airbrakes in, play the g against speed to arrive pointing at crowd centre at 380 kts. Pull up to the vertical — reheat lit and quarter roll onto display axis . . . keep pulling to complete the loop. Over the top at 4700 ft, cancel reheat pulling through the vertical and crank into wind slightly to maintain display

axis. Pull into vertical at display centre, reheat in and, once vertical, half-roll and pull over into the second loop of a horizontal eight. Again cancel reheat coming down, and level at 250 ft.

'Now we can show the tight turn radius by doing a decelerating turn and dropping the landing gear and flap down the 360° circle. That brings us back to crowd centre in the landing configuration — a slow speed fly-by, followed by a clean up and a reheat rotation into the vertical. If we barrel-roll away from the crowd during the climb and then allow the nose to drop we can complete a wing-over back onto the display line for a classic slow roll. Speed around 380 kts and lots of top rudder to yaw the nose up as we roll, swap the rudder over as we invert and gently ease through the roll to the upright position again. All the time watching the altimeter like a hawk — the reading doesn't matter so long as the needle remains steady at the entry height. Pull up and away for a Derry-wing over and drop onto the display axis for a straight loop. Pulling up at 380 kts and hitting the R/H at the pull will give a tight 4½ g loop — remembering to push level as we reach the zenith to make the loop round and not egg-shaped. Adjust for wind over the top and pull out at the bottom for a reverse wing-over for an inverted run. Stick forward, pushing − 1½ g to keep level, restricting rpm to spin out the inverted time. Now 270° roll round to a hard turn away from the crowd to make room to build up speed for the high speed exit. Reheat in early and ease down to 250 ft, building the speed to the airshow permitted maximum of Mach 0.92. Pull to the vertical and roll through 360° — by easing into a bunt on a good day the aircraft will reach 30,000 ft. Look over the shoulder to see the airfield shrinking below and reflect on how lucky you are to be paid to do the job.'

Below and opposite *XR720, an F 3 of No 11 Squadron demonstrates all its profiles for the cameraman at the 1976 IAT at Greenham Common* (Peter March).

Appendices

1 Lightning production

English Electric Aviation Ltd

P 1A Three prototypes.

WG760 ff R.P. Beamont 4-8-54 Boscombe Down. Dismantled at Warton, 8-62; to Weeton as instructional airframe *7755M;* to St Athan, 9-65; to Henlow as gate guardian, 6-67. Total flights 703, hours flown 268h 17m. Fitted with Sapphire Engines (later with reheat). In care of RAF Binbrook, 10-83.

WG763 ff R.P. Beamont 18-7-55 Warton. First public appearance of P 1 at SBAC Farnborough 1955. To the NAE (later RAE) Bedford Aerodynamics Flight, 21-6-57. First aircraft with guns and 250-gallon ventral tank. To Henlow, 11-65, as instructional airframe *7816M.* Fitted with Sapphire engines without reheat. Air and Space Museum Manchester, 1983.

WG765 Structural test airframe at Warton, never flew.

P 1B Three prototypes.

XA847 ff R.P. Beamont 4-4-57 Warton. Achieved Mach 1.2 on first flight. On 25-11-58 became first British aircraft to fly at Mach 2.0; carried nameplate on port side recording this. To Farnborough 21-4-66 for loose-gravel trials. Fitted with dorsal fin and carried enlarged ventral tank. First aircraft with Avon engines. To RAF Museum mid-1972. Total flights 468, hours flown 205h 30m.

XA853 ff D. de Villiers 5-9-57 Warton. Mostly flown on gun trials and gas-concentration tests. Top of fin lost in accidental canopy ejection. In-flight fire on flight 51 (J. Dell). Dismantled 2-65. Front fuselage to ML Engineering 1-3-65, centre burned at Boscombe Down, struck off charge (SOC), 10-2-65, wings

returned to Warton for destruction tests. Total flights 296, hours flown 153h 25m. Last flight 3-5-63.

XA856 ff R.P. Beamont 3-1-58 Warton. Used by Rolls Royce for Avon development flying. Delivered to Hucknall 24-3-58 (35th Flt Pilot J. Heyworth) SOC 6-67. Total Flights 296.

P 1B Pre-production batch, 20 aircraft.

XG307 ff R.P. Beamont 3-4-58 Samlesbury. First aircraft built at Samlesbury; to Boscombe Down 24-2-64; to Bedford dump 7-71; derelict.

XG308 ff R.P. Beamont 16-5-58 Samlesbury. To Bedford 29-6-66. Bedford fire dump, 4-72.

XG309 ff D. de Villiers 23-6-58 Samlesbury. To Bedford 6-4-65; to Farnborough 12-7-66; dismantled at Farnborough, 3-67; to R.J. Coley for scrap 27-6-68.

XG310 ff J.W.C. Squier 17-7-58 Samlesbury. Carried out spin-trials programme; Farnborough SBAC show 1963 as a Mk 3. First flight as F 3 16-6-62. Used for taxi testing after being grounded 13-7-64. Long-term storage at Warton until 12-6-68, when stripped by 60 MU. To Shoeburyness 24-6-68 and 30-6-68. Scrapped at AWRE, 1971; nose section to scrapyard in Basildon 28-12-72. This aircraft was first to fly with taller production fin and square top (F 3 Fin). Total flights 374, hours flown 192h 7 mins. Last flight 25-6-64.

XG311 ff D. de Villiers 20-10-58 Samlesbury. Only development-batch aircraft to retain small fin throughout its life. From Shorts, Belfast, to Aden for tropical trials 7-61 to 10-61. Crashed in sea off coast near Warton on 31-7-63, when undercarriage failed to lower. Pilot, D.M. Knight, ejected safely. Total flights 238, hours flown 140h 10m. Last flight 31-7-63.

XG312 ff J.W.C. Squier 29-12-58 Samlesbury. Used by Ferranti for radar trials, mostly at Bitteswell. Forward windscreen shattered on 12-10-66 at Mach 0.9, 37,000 ft; J. Cockburn landed aircraft. Aircraft not flown again, taken to Shoeburyness 14-8-64. SOC 4-72. Total flights 429, hours flown 303h 53m. Last flight 12-10-66.

XG313 ff R.P. Beamont 2-2-59 Samlesbury. To Boscombe Down 28-6-65 for 2-in rocket trials; sold to Airwork Services as instructional airframe; last flight from Boscombe to Sydenham 25-4-68. Became *G27-115* and shipped to Saudi Arabia. Total flights 560, hours flown 351h 17m.

XG325 ff J.W.C. Squier 26-2-59 Samlesbury. Used by De Havilland for Firestreak Trials; SOC at Warton, 3-66; dismantled by 60 MU stored at Shoeburyness 28-10-68. Front fuselage used as demonstration unit by 1476 Squadron ATC. Total flights 282, hours flown 221h 2m.

XG326 ff P. Hillwood 14-3-59 Samlesbury. Stored at Warton from 6-10-67; dismantled by 60 MU and shipped to Shoeburyness 10-6-68. Displayed on Horseguards Parade for BoB Display on 50th Anniversary of RAF in 1968. SOC 1971. Total flights 551, hours flown 416h 2m.

XG327 ff J.W.C. Squier 10-4-59 Samlesbury. Last of original batch of development aircraft to be used at Warton, mainly on radar trials. Cat 4 damage at Boscombe on 20-2-60. Modified to F 3 standard. To Bedford for supersonic noise tests, stored 8-71; to St Athan as instructional airframe *8188M* mid-72. No ventral tank fitted. At Manston, 1981.

XG328 ff R.P. Beamont 18-6-59 Samlesbury. OR 946 and Auto-attack trials' aircraft. RAE Bedford, 7-67; AWRE 14-8-68; Farnborough scrap compound 5-72; West Bromwich scrapyard 5-4-73. Total flights 220, hours flown 127h 37m. Last flight 20-1-66.

XG329 ff R.P. Beamont 30-4-59 Samlesbury. Mainly used on gun-firing programme; used by de Havilland from 6-4-66 to 21-12-66; to Cranwell Engineering School 1970 as *8050M*.

XG330 ff J.W.C. Squier 30-6-59 Samlesbury. OR946 trials aircraft, used for fire-zone trials. To fire dump at Warton, then to scrap dealer in Chorley in 1970. Hours flown 170h 24m. Last flight 5-1-65.

XG331 ff J.W.C. Squier 14-5-59 Samlesbury. Damaged at Warton after No 1 engine's starter exploded. Rebuilt. Used for tropical trials in Aden, 7-60; to Shoeburyness in parts on 26-6, 8-7 and 16-7-68. In scrap yard in Basildon, 28-12-72. Total flights 290, hours flown 196h 14m.

XG332 ff J.W.C. Squier 29-5-59 Samlesbury. Used throughout flying life by the BAC and de Havilland for Firestreak and Red Top trials. Crashed at Hatfield on Red Top programme, 13-9-62. Pilot, G. Aird ejected but injured on landing. This aircraft is featured in the famous photograph of pilot's ejection watched by tractor driver. Total flights 214, hours flown 138h 52m. Last flight 13-9-62.

XG333 ff T.M.S. Ferguson 26-9-59 Samlesbury. First aircraft with Liquid Oxygen system. Shipped to Aden for trials 7-61 to 10-61. Used for Boeing-type rain-repellent programme.

XG334 ff J.W.C. Squier 14-7-59 Samlesbury. To the AFDS, Coltishall, 23-12-59, aircraft 'A'. Crashed, 5-3-60, near Wells-next-the-Sea when undercarriage failed to lower. Pilot, Sqn Leader Harding, ejected safely. Total flights 34, hours flown 23h 35m.

XG335 ff T.M.S. Ferguson 7-8-59 Samlesbury. Aircraft 'B' of the AFDS, Coltishall, 3-60. To Boscombe Down, 12-11-62. Crashed, 11-1-65, in Larkhill Ranges, Wilts (16:18 hrs) after undercarriage malfunction. Pilot, Sqn Ldr J. Whittaker, ejected safely. Total flights 286, hours flown 204h 26m.

XG336 ff J.W.C. Squier 25-8-59 Samlesbury. To the AFDS, Coltishall, as aircraft 'C', 12-59. To Boscombe Down, 6-11-67. To RAF Cosford (?) (sic, in original record card) as instructional airframe *8091M*, 5-70; to Halton, 11-72.

XG337 ff J.K. Isherwood 5-9-59 Samlesbury. Used mainly on Red Top trials at Warton and Boscombe Down. Became *8056M* used at Cosford and Halton. Total flights 698.

Two prototype T 4s Company designation P 11

XL628 ff R.P. Beamont 6-5-59 Warton. First two-seat trainer aircraft. Crashed in Irish Sea, 1-10-59. Pilot, J.W.C. Squier, ejected safely but suffered from exposure. Suspected fin collapse at high Mach number. Total flights 94, hours flown 40h 51m.

XL629 ff R.P. Beamont 29-9-59 Warton. After loss of *XL628*, bore brunt of two-seater development. To the ETPS, Farnborough, 13-5-66, to Boscombe Down 20-12-67. Gate guardian, 1981.

Production batch 20 F 1.

XM134 ff R.P. Beamont 3-11-59 Samlesbury. To Boscombe Down, 31-3-60; to the AFDS, Coltishall, 7-60; to Warton for development flying, 10-11-60; to 74 Squadron, Coltishall, 2-9-63 as aircraft 'A'; to OCU, 1964. Crashed off the Wash, 11-9-64. Pilot, Flt Lt Bond, ejected safely. Remains at Farnborough, 10-64, and Warton, 5-66. Total hours 229h 15m.

XM135 ff T.M.S. Ferguson 14-11-59 Samlesbury. To the Central Fighter Establishment, Coltishall, 25-5-60 as aircraft 'D'; to 74 Squadron as 'B'; to 226 OCU, 9-63; to Leuchars Target Facilities Flight; to 60 MU, 28-6-71. To IWM collection, Duxford, 20-11-74. Total hours, 1343h.

XM136 ff J.C. Hall 1-12-59 Samlesbury. To the CFE, 'E', 21-6-60; to 74 Squadron, 'C', 15-11-62; to 226 OCU 9-64; to Wattisham TFF 'B', 8-66. Crashed near Coltishall, 13-9-67, after reheat fire followed by loss of tailplane control. Pilot ejected safely.

XM137 ff J.K. Isherwood 14-12-59 Samlesbury. To the CFE, Coltishall, 28-6-60, 'F'; to 74 Squadron 2-10-62, 'D', later 'T'; to 226 OCU 9-64; to 33 MU, then to Binbrook TFF, 15-3-66, 'Y'; to 23 Squadron and Leuchars TFF; to Wattisham TFF, 'Y', 1970; to Leuchars TFF 18-1-71; to 60 MU 11-73; at Leconfield 20-7-74; to 60 MU used in storage tests. Total hours 766h 25m.

XM138 ff J.K. Isherwood 23-12-59 Samlesbury. To the CFE, Coltishall, 30-6-60, 'G'; to 74 Squadron 16-12-60, caught fire on landing, pilot Flt Lt Hopkins unhurt, Cat 4 damage, never repaired; to Coltishall fire dump, 10-66. Nose on Farnborough firing range, 11-72. Total hours 714h 35m.

XM139 ff D. de Villiers 12-1-60 Samlesbury. To 74 Squadron 2-8-60, 'C', later 'F'. To OCU, 9-64; to Leuchars (Marked Royal Scottish Air Force), 8-65; to Wattisham TFF then to 33 MU; to Warton for Cat 4 wing change, 14-11-69, before becoming official RAF Fighter Display Aircraft, returned to Wattisham 19-2-70. Used by Flt Lt R. Pengelly at SBAC Farnborough 70 and 72, Paris Air Show 71. Became *8411M* at Wattisham 1981.

XM140 ff D. de Villiers 25-1-60 Samlesbury. To 74 Squadron 2-8-60 'M'; to OCU, 9-63; to 111 Squadron, 1-65, reduced to spares at 33 MU Lyneham 10-66.

XM141 ff J.C. Hall 9-2-60 Samlesbury. To 74 Squadron 29-8-60, 'D'; to OCU, 9-63. Damaged in take-off accident 16-5-61; to 33 MU, Lyneham, and reduced to spares, 8-66. Fuselage returned to Warton but sold for scrap, 14-1-72.

XM142 ff T.M.S. Ferguson 19-2-60 Samles-

bury. To 74 Squadron, 30-8-60, 'B'. Crashed in sea off Cromer 26-4-63, after control failure. Pilot, Flt Lt T.M. Burns, ejected safely.

XM143 ff J.K. Isherwood 27-2-60 Samlesbury. To 74 Squadron, 15-9-60, 'A'; to OCU, 9-63, reduced to spares at 33 MU Lyneham, 8-66.

XM144 ff T.M.S. Ferguson 14-3-60 Samlesbury. To 74 Squadron, 30-9-60, 'J' and 'G'; to OCU, 9-63; Cat 3 accident 29-9-64, repaired; then to Leconfield TFF; to 60 MU, 17-6-65, for storage; to Wattisham TFF 'B'; then to Leuchars TFF 'X'; to 23 Squadron 4-72; then to 60 MU as 'hack', before becoming *8417M*. Gate guardian, Leuchars, 1981.

XM145 ff D. de Villiers 18-3-60 Samlesbury. To 74 Squadron, 14-5-62, possibly TFF 'Q' and 'H'. Damaged in Cat 3 landing accident at Coltishall, 19-8-63, repaired; then to 226 OCU and the Leuchars TFF, 9-66. In storage at 60 MU until mid-73.

XM146 ff J.C. Hall 29-3-60 Samlesbury. To 74 Squadron, 'L', 4-9-60; to 226 OCU, 9-63. To 111 Squadron, 'J'; scrapped at 33 MU Lyneham, 11-66.

XM147 ff T.M.S. Ferguson 7-4-60 Samlesbury. To the AFDS, Coltishall, 'G', 3-9-60; to 74 Squadron, 'P' and 'J'; to 56 Squadron TFF; Cat 3 damage repaired at 33 MU; then stored at 60 MU, 3-4-70; to Binbrook TFF, Cat 3 damage twice at Binbrook, involving replacement of wings on one occasion and fin/rudder after loss in flight, on another. Wattisham TFF, 6-72; Leuchars, 6-73; Wattisham TFF, 9-73; then became instructional airframe *8412M*.

XM163 ff D. de Villiers 23-4-60 Samlesbury. To the AFDS, as 'H', 4-11-60; to 74 Squadron, 'Q', 6-61; to 226 OCU, 9-64; Wattisham TFF, 8-68. 60 MU, 7-69; Wattisham TFF 'A', 8-70; to 60 MU for storage, 16-2-72.

XM164 ff D. de Villiers 13-6-60 Samlesbury. To Boscombe Down, then to 74 Squadron, 'K', 8-60; to 226 OCU, 9-64; then to 33 MU and to Fighter Command Trials unit (later renamed Binbrook TFF), 22-2-64; to 60 MU, 3-69, and to Leuchars, 9-71; to 60 MU for storage, 4-72.

XM165 ff R.P. Beamont 30-5-60 Samlesbury. First aircraft to enter RAF Squadron service as 'A' of 74 Squadron, 29-6-60. To 226 OCU, 10-63. Scrapped at 33 MU Lyneham, 10-66.

XM166 ff T.M.S. Ferguson 1-7-60 Samlesbury. To 74 Squadron, 'G' 2-8-60; to 226 OCU, 9-63, scrapped by 33 MU Lyneham, 10-66.

XM167 ff J.C. Hall 14-7-60 Samlesbury. To 74 Squadron, 'H', 26-9-60. Cat 3 damage on unknown date; to 226 OCU, then to 33 MU for storage. SOC 10-66. Total flights 681, hours flown, 525h 55m.

XM168 Structural test airframe, never flown, used for tests at Warton.

Lightning F 1A 24 built.

XM169 ff R.P. Beamont 16-8-60 Samlesbury. First F 1A and first aircraft to be fitted with production refuelling probe, used for trials on flight refuelling. To 111 Squadron, Wattisham, 14-10-64. Stored at 33 MU then to Binbrook TFF. Instructional airframe *8422M* at Leuchars in 1981.

XM170 ff J.K. Isherwood 12-9-60 Samlesbury. This aircraft made only one flight and was scrapped after being contaminated by mercury during pre-flight tests. Used in Lord Mayor's Show London 1961 or 62. To Newton as *7877M* 11-65. Scrapped at Swinderby, 10-66. Total flying time 14m.

XM171 ff R.P. Beamont 20-9-60 Samlesbury. To Boscombe Down, 10-11-60; to 56 Squadron, Wattisham, 28-2-61 as 'R' and 'A'. Collided with *XM179*, 6-6-63, landed safely. To OCU then to 60 MU, 11-9-73. SOC, 25-3-74.

XM172 ff J.K. Isherwood 10-10-60 Samlesbury. To 56 Squadron as 'B', 14-12-60. First F 1A in RAF service; to OCU and became *8427M* gate guardian, Coltishall, 1981.

XM173 ff J.K. Isherwood 1-11-60 Samlesbury. To 56 Squadron as 'C', 2-1-61. Instructional airframe *8414M*. Gate guardian, Bentley Priory, 1981.

XM174 ff J.K. Isherwood 15-11-60 Samlesbury. To 56 Squadron, 'D', 15-12-60; Cat 4 damage, 19-11-63; to OCU Coltishall; to Leuchars TFF. Crashed into a quarry at Bulmullo on approach to Leuchars, 29-11-68. Pilot ejected safely. Total hours, 1262h 25m.

XM175 ff D. de Villiers 23-11-60 Samlesbury. To 56 Squadron as 'E', 21-12-60; to 60 MU, 12-67; to Warton for spares mid-73. Total hours, 771h 5m.

XM176 ff J.K. Isherwood 1-12-60 Samlesbury. To 56 Squadron, 16-1-61. Caught fire on ground at Wattisham, 14-2-61. To 60 MU, 12-67.

XM177 ff R.P. Beamont 20-12-60 Samlesbury. To 56 Squadron, 28-2-61; to OCU Coltishall and to Wattisham TFF; to 60 MU: broken up, 3-74.

XM178 ff J.K. Isherwood 30-12-60 Samlesbury. To 56 Squadron and OCU Coltishall. *8418M* at Leuchars, 1981.

XM179 ff D. de Villiers 4-1-61 Samlesbury. To 56 Squadron, 'J', 28-2-61. Collided with *XM171*, 6-6-63, during formation fly-past and bomb-burst, wreckage landed at Great Bricett. Pilot, Flt Lt Cook, ejected but was seriously injured. Total flying time 352h 55m.

XM180 ff D. de Villiers 23-1-61 Samlesbury. To 56 Squadron, Wattisham and Coltishall OCU. *8424M* 1981.

XM181 ff R.P. Beamont 25-1-61 Samlesbury. To 111 Squadron, Wattisham, 29-9-61; to 56 Squadron, 5-63. Caught fire on engine run, became *8415M* at Binbrook, 1981.

XM182 ff T.M.S. Ferguson 6-2-61 Samlesbury. To 56 Squadron, 'P', 13-3-61; to OCU Coltishall and to Leuchars TFF 9-74. *8425M* 1981.

XM183 ff R.P. Beamont 9-2-61 Samlesbury. To 56 Squadron, 6-3-61; to OCU Coltishall and became *8416M* at Binbrook, 1981.

XM184 ff T.M.S. Ferguson 9-2-61 Samlesbury. To 111 Squadron, 13-4-61. Caught fire on landing at Coltishall, 17-4-67 (Flt Lt Crumbie) Cat 5 write-off. Total hours 1013h 40m.

XM185 ff R.P. Beamont 9-2-61 Samlesbury. To 56 Squadron, 6-3-61. Crashed 28-6-61 after hydraulic failure. Pilot, Flying Officer P. Ginger ejected safely. Total hours 39h 25m.

XM186 ff T.M.S. Ferguson 14-3-61 Samlesbury. To 111 Squadron, 13-4-61. Crashed on take-off at Wittering, 18-7-63. Entered cloud on wing-over, failed to recover, pilot, Flt Lt Gartside killed. Total hours 420h 40m. 488 Flights.

XM187 ff D. de Villiers 20-3-61 Samlesbury. To 111 Squadron, 24-4-61. Instructional airframe *7838M* at Newton, 11-65.

XM188 ff J.K. Isherwood 27-3-61 Samlesbury. This aircraft was flown by South African Air Force personnel at Warton before going to 111 Squadron on 31-5-61. Believed to be Cat 5 damaged when brake failure caused it to collide with squadron office.

XM189 ff D. de Villiers 30-3-61 Samlesbury. Flown on 11 flights by USAF personnel at Warton before delivery to 111 Squadron, 1-5-61. Damaged in taxying accident, 19-1-62. To OCU, 6-72, in 65 Squadron markings. Instructional airframe *8423 M*, 1981.

XM190 ff T.M.S. Ferguson 1-5-61 Samlesbury. Evaluated at Warton by Indian Air Force, to 111 Squadron, 20-6-61. To 226 OCU. Crashed in sea off Cromer, 15-3-66.

Pilot, Capt Peterson USAF, ejected safely. Aircraft salvaged, 25-4-66, landed at Great Yarmouth. Total flights 1019, hours flown 853h 30m.

XM191 ff T.M.S. Ferguson 8-5-61 Samlesbury. To 111 Squadron, 28-6-61. Crashed Wattisham, 9-6-64, after fire on take-off which destroyed rear fuselage by time aircraft landed. Pilot, Flt Lt N. Smith, not injured. Front fuselage to 71 MU, became *7854M*. Total flights 613, hours flown 554h 35m.

XM192 ff J.K. Isherwood 25-5-61 Samlesbury. To 111 Squadron as 'K', 28-6-61. Gate guardian, Wattisham, 1981. *8413M*

XM213 ff J.K. Isherwood 3-6-61 Samlesbury. To 111 Squadron, 30-6-61. Crashed on take-off at Coltishall, 6-5-66. Pilot, Sqn Ldr Hobley, not injured, aircraft written off. Total hours 885h 35m.

XM214 ff J.K. Isherwood 29-6-61 Samlesbury. To 111 Squadron, 1-8-61, after fuel problem on initial delivery flight of 28-7-61. First aircraft with standard brake chute attachment system. *8420M*, 1981.

XM215 ff D. de Villiers 11-7-61 Samlesbury. To 111 Squadron, 2-8-61; to OCU and Binbrook TFF. *8421M*, 1981.

XM216 ff T.M.S. Ferguson Samlesbury. To 111 Squadron, 29-8-61. Engine starter exploded at Coltishall, 24-6-65; repaired at Warton, returned to OCU 7-9-66. *8426M*, 1981

XM217 Serial allocated but aircraft not built.

XM218 Serial allocated but aircraft not built.

Lightning T 4 20 built

XM966 ff R.P. Beamont 15-7-60 Samlesbury. First flight as T 4 to Filton for T 5 conversion; second T 5 to fly. Crashed on test flight over Irish Sea, 22-7-65, after loss of fin. J.L. Dell and G. Elkington ejected safely. Aircraft salvaged. Total flights 263 and hours 152h 51 m.

XM967 ff J.L. Dell 30-3-62 Bristol. First T 5 to fly. To Farnborough, 22-5-68, became *8433M*; on fire dump at Kemble, 12-76.

XM968 ff R.P. Beamont 9-11-60 Samlesbury. Used for T 4 Appraisal and development flying, also as chase aircraft for TSR2. Used by OCU and 56 Squadron, became *8541M*.

XM969 ff J.L. Dell 28-3-61 Warton. Used for 70 development flights at Warton before going to OCU at Middleton St George. Burned on Binbrook fire dump in 1982 as *8592M*.

XM970 ff T.M.S. Ferguson 5-5-61 Warton. Used for 26 development flights at Warton before going to OCU at Middleton St George,

2-11-61. First T 4 in RAF service. Used at 1962 Paris Air Show; became *8529M*.

XM971 ff J.K. Isherwood 23-6-61 Samlesbury. To Middleton St George, 23-7-62. Crashed near Tunstead, Norfolk, 2-1-67, after debris from intake (bullet) entered engine. Sqn Ldr Carlton and Flt Lt Grose ejected safely. Total hours 688h 30m.

XM972 ff D. de Villiers 29-4-61 Samlesbury. To OCU Middleton St George, 2-7-62.

XM973 ff T.M.S. Ferguson 17-5-61 Samlesbury. Used for 27 development flights at Warton before despatch to 74 Squadron, Coltishall, 3-8-62. Became *8528M*.

XM974 ff T.M.S. Ferguson 19-6-61 Samlesbury. Appeared at 1961 SBAC show; to 74 Squadron, 3-8-62. Crashed into North Sea, 14-12-72, when both reheats and one engine caught fire. Flt Lt Spencer and Plt Off Evans ejected safely. Total hours 1753.

XM987 ff T.M.S. Ferguson 13-7-61 Samlesbury. To OCU at Middleton St George, 20-8-62.

XM988 ff T.M.S. Ferguson 21-8-61 Samlesbury. To OCU Middleton St George, 12-10-62. Crashed North Sea, 5-6-73, when entered into a spin from Mach 1.1 spiral descent. Wing Commander C. Bruce ejected.

XM989 ff T.M.S. Ferguson 30-8-61. Samlesbury. To 56 Squadron, 5-9-62. Bought by the BAC for Saudi Arabian contract, 6-4-66. To Saudi Arabia as T 54, *54-650*, later *54-607*.

XM990 ff R.P. Beamont 21-9-61 Warton. To OCU Middleton St George, 20-9-62. Crashed during BoB Display, 19-9-70. Entered uncontrolled roll at East Plumstead (near Coltishall), and failed to recover. Flt Lts Fuller and Sumskin ejected safely. Hours flown 1282h.

XM991 ff R.P. Beamont 4-10-61 Warton. To OCU at Middleton St George; later to 19 Squadron as 'T'. Damaged at Gütersloh, 3-5-74. Became *8456M*.

XM992 ff R.P. Beamont 13-12-61 Warton. To 111 Squadron Wattisham, 24-9-62. Purchased by the BAC for Saudi Arabian contract, 7-4-66; to Saudi Arabia, 6-6-66, as T 54 coded *54-651*, later *54-608*. Cat 3 starter fire at Khamis Mushayt, 26-10-70.

XM993 ff J.K. Isherwood 9-12-61 Samlesbury. To OCU at Middleton St George, 4-10-62. Crashed at Middleton St George, 12-12-62, when it ran off runway and was burned out. No casualties.

XM994 ff D. de Villiers 12-3-62 Warton. To 19 Squadron at Leconfield, 6-11-62.

XM995 ff D. de Villiers 25-1-62 Warton. To 92 Squadron as 'T', 29-11-62. Became *8542M*.
XM996 ff T.M.S. Ferguson 13-4-62 Samlesbury. To OCU Middleton St George, 8-1-63.
XM997 ff D. de Villiers 22-5-62 Samlesbury. To OCU Middleton St George, 14-1-63.

Lightning F 2 44 Built.
XN723 ff J.L. Dell 11-7-61 Samlesbury. To Boscombe Down for appraisal 6-2-62; to Rolls Royce, 2-4-63. Crashed at Hucknall while with Rolls Royce, due to fire in No 2 engine bay. Mr D. Withnal ejected safely.
XN724 ff T.M.S. Ferguson 11-9-61 Samlesbury. To Boscombe Down, 22-5-62; to 33 MU, 5-9-63; to Warton, 20-10-66, for F 2A conversion. To 19 Squadron as 'F'; eventually became *8513 M*.
XN725 ff J.L. Dell 31-3-62 Samlesbury. Converted to F 3 prototype (Avon 301s). First aircraft with cambered leading edge. Carried a variety of test ventral tanks and used at RAE Bedford for Concorde 'noise' and high-speed trials.
XN726 ff J.K. Isherwood 29-9-61 Samlesbury. To the CFE, Binbrook, 14-2-63. Converted to F 2A at Warton; first flight as F 2A, 28-3-68 (J.L. Dell). First F 2A with Avon 211s. To 19 Squadron as 'D', 7-6-68. Cat 4 damage by lightning strike, to Samlesbury by road, 2-6-72. At Farnborough in 1977 as *8545M*.

XN727 ff D. de Villiers 13-10-61 Samlesbury To 92 Squadron as 'A' Leconfield. Converted to F 2A in 1969; at Farnborough as *8547M* in 1977.
XN728 ff T.M.S. Ferguson 26-10-61 Samlesbury. To 92 Squadron as 'B', 1-4-63. Undercarriage collapsed, 3-4-68; during repair converted to F 2A, returned to 92 Squadron as 'F', 24-6-69. Became *8546M*.
XN729 ff T.M.S. Ferguson 3-11-61 Samlesbury. To the AFDS, CFE Binbrook, 1-3-63. Carried out flight-refuelling trials at Wattisham. Bought by the BAC, 7-3-67, to replace crashed Saudi Arabian Mk 52 (*52-657* ex-*XN796*). To Saudi Arabia, 9-5-67, as *52-659*, later *52-612*; crashed, 2-5-70, near Khamis Mushayt.
XN730 ff D. de Villiers 23-11-61 Samlesbury. To 19 Squadron as 'B', 12-3-63. Converted to F 2A and to 92 Squadron, 30-8-68. Became *8496M*.
XN731 ff T.M.S. Ferguson 8-1-62 Samlesbury. To handling squadron, Boscombe Down, 22-4-63; to 92 Squadron, 8-63. Converted to F 2A; first flight 21-3-69; back to 92 Squadron as 'L'; to 19 Squadron as 'Z', 1-73. To 60 MU 19-2-74. Became *8518M*.
XN732 ff J.K. Isherwood 19-1-62 Samlesbury. To 92 Squadron as 'H', 30-4-63. Converted to F 2A and returned to 92 as 'R', 12-8-69. To 60 MU, 3-74. Became *8519M*.

Below *No 92 Squadron's serpent still seems to hold its head up high in a defiant pose, despite the ravages of time on Lightning F 2A XN730's airframe. This derelict is nothing more than a shell, as the ejection seat, armament, ventral tank, engines, nose radar cone and all other vital equipment have been removed* (Bob Downey).

Above *A sad end for a 19 Squadron F 2 at Gütersloh* (R.L. Ward).

Below 8347M *was originally* XN768; *it was one of the few F 2s not converted to F 2A standard* (Bob Downey).

XN733 ff D. de Villiers 1-2-62 Samlesbury. To 92 Squadron as 'L', 6-6-63. Cat 4 damage at Gütersloh after starter explosion, returned to Warton and converted to F 2A, back to 92 as 'R', later 'Y', 31-12-69. Became *8520M*.

XN734 ff D. de Villiers 13-7-62 Samlesbury. Aircraft on charge to Rolls Royce for engine development programme F 3 (Avon 301s). To Hucknall, 6-12-65; returned to Warton, 18-9-67; to 60 MU, 5-2-70. Sold to the BAC for Saudi Arabian contract as *G27-239*.

XN735 ff D. de Villiers 23-2-62 Samlesbury. To 92 Squadron as 'J', 10-5-63; to Warton for F 2A conversion, 30-8-68. To Gütersloh, 25-4-69, 19 Squadron as 'A'. Became *8552M*.

XN767 ff T.M.S. Ferguson 19-2-62 Samlesbury. To 33 MU, Lyneham. Bought by the BAC for Saudi Arabian contract; to Warton, 9-5-66. Dispatched, 22-7-66, as *52-655*, later *52-609*.

XN768 ff T.M.S. Ferguson 14-3-62 Samlesbury. To 33 MU, Lyneham, 5-7-63; to 92 Squadron as 'S', 5-73. Not converted to F 2A. *8347M* on Gütersloh dump, 9-73.

XN769 ff D. de Villiers 31-3-62 Samlesbury. To 33 MU, Lyneham, 5-9-63; to 92 Squadron as 'Z', not converted to F 2A. *8402M* at West Drayton.

XN770 ff T.M.S. Ferguson 24-4-62 Samlesbury. To 33 MU Lyneham, never allocated to a squadron. Bought by the BAC for Saudi Arabian contract; to Warton, 4-5-66, to Saudi Arabia as *52-656*, later *52-610*, 11-7-66.

XN771 ff R.P. Beamont 29-8-62 Samlesbury. To the AFDS, Binbrook as 'M', 14-11-62; to 33 MU; to the CFE; to Warton, 21-9-66, for F 2A conversion; first flight 1-2-68; to 19 Squadron as 'P', 21-3-68.

XN772 ff D. de Villiers 10-5-62 Samlesbury. To Boscombe Down, 7-11-63; to Warton for F 2A conversion. 4-9-67; to Gütersloh, 92 Squadron as 'N', 2-8-68. Crashed, 28-1-71, Flying Officer Hitchcock ejected safely. Hours flown 923h.

XN773 ff D. de Villiers 13-6-62 Samlesbury. To Rolls Royce at Hucknall, 25-5-64; to 60 MU, 3-65; to Warton for F 2A conversion, 10-7-67, to Gütersloh, 92 Squadron as 'E'. Became *8521M*.

XN774 ff D. de Villiers 27-9-62 Samlesbury. To 19 Squadron as 'C', 13-2-63; to Warton for F 2A conversion, 13-8-69. Became *8551M*.

XN775 ff T.M.S. Ferguson 1-10-62 Samlesbury. To 19 Squadron, 17-12-62. First F 2 in RAF service; to Warton for F 2A conversion,

7-6-68; to 92 Squadron as 'B', 15-1-69. Became *8448M*.

XN776 ff D. de Villiers 18-10-62 Samlesbury. To 19 Squadron as 'E'; to Warton for F 2A conversion, 14-1-69; to Gütersloh, 19 Squadron as 'C', 13-8-69.

XN777 ff D. de Villiers 13-7-62 Samlesbury. To the AFDS, Binbrook. Damaged, 21-12-62, when nose leg broke off. To 33 MU, then to Warton for F 2A conversion, 5-10-66. First flight, 2-3-68, then to 19 Squadron as 'K', 26-3-68. Became *8536M*.

XN778 ff T.M.S. Ferguson 9-11-62 Samlesbury. To 19 Squadron, 9-1-63; to Warton for F 2 conversion, 10-5-68; back to 92 Squadron as 'H', 19-12-68. Became *8537M*.

XN779 ff R.P. Beamont 20-11-62 Samlesbury. To 19 Squadron 'G', 27-2-63; to Warton, 11-3-66, for Cat 4 repair; returned to Germany, 2-2-67; to 60 MU, 10-69. With 19 Squadron as 'X', 8-7-71. Gütersloh dump, 9-73. *8348M*.

XN780 ff D. de Villiers 7-12-62 Samlesbury To 19 Squadron, 12-2-63. To Warton for F 2A conversion, 27-2-68; to 19 Squadron as 'H'; then to 92 Squadron as 'G' and 'K', 4-10-68.

XN781 ff T.M.S. Ferguson 12-12-62 Samlesbury. To 19 Squadron, Leconfield, as 'J', 15-3-63, to 33 MU, then to Warton, 13-9-66, for F 2A conversion. First flight, 29-12-67; to 19 Squadron as 'B', 26-2-68. Became *8538M*.

XN782 ff R.P. Beamont 20-12-62 Samlesbury. To 19 Squadron as 'K', 19-2-63; to Warton for F 2A conversion, 27-3-68; returned to Germany, 25-11-68, as 'H', 92 Squadron. Became *8539M*.

XN783 ff D. de Villiers 26-1-63 Samlesbury. To 92 Squadron as 'A'. Cat 3 damaged, 16-11-65. To Warton for F 2A conversion, 1-5-69; to 19 Squadron as 'G'. Became *8526M*.

XN784 ff J. K. Isherwood 26-1-63 Samlesbury. To 19 Squadron, 19-3-63; to Warton for F 2A conversion, 30-1-69; returned to 19 Squadron as 'L', later 'R'. Became *8540M*.

XN785 ff J.K. Isherwood 30-1-63 Samlesbury. To 19 Squadron, 5-4-63, as 'C'. Crashed near Diffield, 27-4-64 after flight-refuelling exercise, attempted to land at disused airfield, Hutton Cranswick. Flying Officer Davey did not eject and was killed. Hours flown 285h 55m.

XN786 ff T.M.S. Ferguson 12-2-63 Samlesbury. To 92 Squadron as 'D', 9-4-63. Cat 3 damage, 3-8-65. To Warton, 29-10-68, for F 2A conversion, returned to 19 Squadron as 'M'. First Lightning to carry definitive camouflage

Above *Despite being virtually consigned to the scrap heap, these No 92 Squadron Lightnings are still performing a vital role at Gütersloh where they act as decoys. All photographs in this sequence were taken on September 16 1982. The Phantom motif behind the squadron marking, on the nearest aircraft, no doubt records earlier moments of glory* (Bob Downey).

Below and right *Starboard side of XN786, which at first glance seems to be reasonably intact, apart from pitot head and jet pipes. Compare this with port view opposite . . . panels have been removed, some are loose, and the ejection seat is no longer in the cockpit. Instructional airframe number 8500M was allocated to this particular Lightning* (Bob Downey).

Above right *XN786 'M' is a No 19 Squadron F 2A, whereas the 92 Squadron aircraft in the foreground is an F 2. It is a great pity that the latter's serial number cannot be clearly read; it looks as if it is XN782, but this aircraft was converted to F 2A standard on November 25 1968 and became 8539M. The only two F 2s not converted to F 2A, and not accounted for, were not at Gütersloh in 1982* (Bob Downey).

Above *Two 92 Squadrons F 2s finish their days pushed into a corner at Gütersloh like discarded playthings. No doubt to Russian reconnaissance aircraft they still appear to be part of NATO's front line fighter force* (Bob Downey).

scheme in 5-72. Became *8500M*.

XN787 ff T.M.S. Ferguson 15-2-63 Samlesbury. To 19 Squadron as 'M', 22-3-63; to Warton, 1-7-69, for F 2A conversion; then to 92 Squadron as 'L'. At 60 MU, 7-73, became *8522M*.

XN788 ff R.P. Beamont 25-2-53 Samlesbury. To 92 Squadron as 'P', 23-5-63; on loan to 111 Squadron, 25-5-64£ 3-7-64; became 'R' on return to 92. To Warton, 12-8-69, for F 2A conversion; to 92 Squadron as 'P'; to 60 MU, 15-2-73. Port main gear collapsed, 29-5-74, at Gütersloh when brake 'chute failed. *8543M*.

XN789 ff D. de Villiers 11-3-63 Samlesbury. To 92 Squadron as 'G', 26-4-63; to 33 MU, 9-66; to Warton, 5-9-66, for F 2A conversion; to 19 Squadron, 15-1-68, as 'J'. *8527M*.

XN790 ff J.K. Isherwood 20-3-63. Samlesbury. To 92 Squadron, 25-4-63; to Warton, 26-5-68, for F 2A conversion; to 19 Squadron as 'L',

30-1-69. *8523M*.

XN791 ff R.P. Beamont 4-4-63 Samlesbury. To 19 Squadron as 'N', 15-5-63; to Warton, 21-3-68, for F 2A conversion; to Germany, 92 Squadron 29-10-68, as 'D'. *8524M*.

XN792 ff R.P. Beamont 19-4-63 Samlesbury. To 92 Squadron as 'N', 24-6-63; to Warton, 2-8-68, for F 2A conversion; to Gütersloh, 92 Squadron as 'M', 21-3-69; to 60 MU, 17-8-73. *8525M*.

XN793 ff D. de Villiers 1-5-63 Samlesbury. To 92 Squadron as 'K', 21-6-63; to Warton, 26-9-68, for F 2A conversion; to 92 Squadron as 'A', 1-5-69. Damaged at Gütersloh, 18-9-73. *8544M*.

XN794 ff T.M.S. Ferguson 16-5-63 Samlesbury. Damaged by fire on second engine run. To 33 MU, 5-9-63; to 19 Squadron, 1966, to 92 Squadron as 'R', 2-71. Not converted to F 2A. *8349M*.

XN795 ff J. Carrodus 30-5-63 Samlesbury. To 33 MU, 13-7-63; to Warton, 9-7-64, for F 2A conversion. First F 2A conversion — only fin and tank modified, wing as F 2. In storage at Warton; to Boscombe Down, 12-11-68; to Warton in 1972 for MRCA Development Flying (27 mm Mauser gun trials) with the BAC on MoD contract work, 1982.

XN796 ff D. de Villiers 12-7-63 Samlesbury. To 33 MU, 11-10-63; never allocated to RAF squadron. Bought by the BAC for Saudi Arabian contract; to Warton, 29-4-66; to Saudi as *52-657*, 8-7-66. Crashed on take-off, 20-9-66, after excessive rotation at low airspeed. Pilot not injured, but aircraft written off.

XN797 ff T.M.S. Ferguson 5-9-63 Samlesbury. To 33 MU, 4-10-63; never allocated to RAF squadron. Bought by the BAC for Saudi Arabian contract. To Warton, 28-4-66; to Saudi as *52-658*, later *52-611*, 22-7-66. Crashed 29-11-68 at Khamis Mushayt — stalled when practising single-engine approaches. Major S. Ghimlas killed.

British Aircraft Corporation Ltd (Preston Division)
Lightning F 3 Production batch, 70 built.

XP693 ff J.L. Dell 16-6-62. Samlesbury. Converted to Mk 3A standard used on development-batch programme. To Boscombe Down, 1-11-67; to Warton, 19-1-68. MRCA trials (avionics), 1972, and gun trials at Boscombe Down, 1974. With MoD(PE) Warton, 1981; with 5 and 11 Squadrons, Binbrook, 1983.

XP694 ff R.P. Beamont 1-5-63 Samlesbury. Used on F 3 DB programme; to Boscombe Down 4-7-64 for F 3 appraisal. Used by Ferranti for AI23B programme. To full F 3 standard before dispatch to 60 MU. To 29 Squadron and then to Binbrook with the LAF and No 11 Squadron, 1983.

XP695 ff R.P. Beamont 20-6-63 Samlesbury. To the CFE Binbrook, 1-1-64; to Warton, 3-7-67, for full F 3 mods. To 111 Squadron (L), 9-72. 11 Squadron Binbrook, 1983.

XP696 ff J.L. Dell 2-7-63 Samlesbury. To the CFE, Binbrook, 15-1-64; to Boscombe Down for Red Top trials, 16-2-66 to 5-6-67; to Warton for full F 3 modifications; to 226 OCU, 8-72.

XP697 ff D. M. Knight 18-7-63 Samlesbury. First flight minus ventral tank. To Bristol for full F 6 conversion, 13-8-63; first flight as F 6, 17-4-64 (R.P. Beamont). Used on programme for 2-in rocket and large ventral-tank tests, and over-wing-tank support programme. MoD(PE) Warton, 1981, static tests.

XP698 ff T.M.S. Ferguson 28-8-63 Samlesbury. To Boscombe Down, 5-3-64; then to 56 and 29 Squadrons. Mid-air collision at night with *XP747* on 16-2-72. Crashed in sea 40 miles east of Ipswich; Flt Lt P. Reynolds ejected safely. Hours flown 1360h.

XP699 ff D. de Villiers 2-9-63 Samlesbury. To Boscombe Down, 10-4-64; to Wheelus Air Force Base on F 3 Tropical Trials. Crashed near Wethersfield, 3-3-67, on flight from Wattisham. Flying Officer Pearse ejected safely. Total flights 367, hours flown 299h 30m.

XP700 ff D. de Villiers 6-6-63 Samlesbury. To 74 Squadron 14-4-64 (A); to 29 Squadron 7-72. Crashed, 7-8-72, damaged tail bumper and ventral tank on take-off. Flt Lt E. Fenton ejected. Wreckage landed at Newton Nr Sudbury. Hours flown 1653h 15m.

XP701 ff T.M.S. Ferguson 14-9-63 Samlesbury. Used on undercarriage tests prior to introduction of Modification 4051. To 29 Squadron, 8-9-67; to 111 Squadron. Code BN with 11 Squadron, 1983, Binbrook. This aircraft had a long history of intake vibration, eventually traced to loose ballast weights in nose.

XP702 ff D. de Villiers 19-9-63 Samlesbury. To 74 Squadron, 14-5-64; then to 56 Squadron, 60 MU and 29 Squadron. At Binbrook, 1983.

XP703 ff D. de Villiers 28-9-63 Samlesbury. To 74 Squadron, 8-6-64; then to 29 Squadron in 1972; MoD(PE) Warton, 1981.

XP704 ff R.P. Beamont 17-10-63 Samlesbury. To 74 Squadron (H), 15-6-64. Crashed at Leuchars, 28-8-64, while practising aerobatics. Pilot, Flt Lt Owen, killed. Hours flown 36h 40m.

XP705 ff D. de Villiers 12-10-63 Samlesbury. To 74 Squadron, then to 23 Squadron (K) and 29 Squadron (L). Crashed in sea 35 miles from Akrotiri, 8-7-71; Flt Lt Clarke ejected safely. Hours flown 1854h.

XP706 ff T.M.S. Ferguson 28-10-63 Samlesbury. To 74 Squadron, 13-7-64; to 111 Squadron (F), 1972. 11 Squadron, Binbrook, 1981.

XP707 ff R.P. Beamont 13-11-63 Samlesbury. To 23 Squadron, 18/19-8-64. With *XP708*, first Lightnings for 23 Squadron. To 226 OCU; then storage at Filton in 1974; with 11 Squadron, Binbrook, 1983.

XP708 ff R.P. Beamont 20-11-63 Samlesbury. See *XP707*. To 29 Squadron (N) in 1972.

XP735 ff R.P. Beamont 4-12-63 Samlesbury. To 23 Squadron, 17-9-64; to 29 Squadron (J). Overshot into barrier, due to brake failure, 13-5-74.

XP736 ff D. de Villiers 13-12-63 Samlesbury. To 23 Squadron; then to 29 Squadron (G). Crashed into sea off Cromer, 22-9-71; pilot, Flg Off Mottershead, killed. Hours flown 1510h.

XP737 ff R.P. Beamont 1-1-64 Samlesbury. To 23 Squadron, 21-10-64. To BAC Filton for storage, 2-9-74.

XP739 ff T.M.S. Ferguson 20-1-64. Samlesbury. To 33 MU, 12-11-64; then to 111 Squadron. Crashed near Wattisham at Battisford, 29-9-65. Flt Lt Molland ejected safely. Hours flown 176h 45m.

XP740 ff D. de Villiers 1-2-64 Samlesbury. To 111 Squadron, 30-12-64. Cat 4 damage at Binbrook, 1-70; back to 111 Squadron after repair.

XP741 ff R.P. Beamont 4-2-64 Samlesbury. To 111 Squadron (D), 22-12-64. With 11 Group, 1981.

XP742 ff D.M. Knight 12-2-64 Samlesbury. To 111 Squadron, 10-2-65. Crashed in sea, east of Great Yarmouth, 7-5-70. Flying Officer Tulloch ejected safely. Hours flown 1258h.

XP743 ff D. de Villiers 18-2-64. Samlesbury. To 33 MU, 18-2-65.

XP744 ff R.P. Beamont 25-2-64 Samlesbury. To 33 MU, 9-3-65; to 56 Squadron. Crashed in sea near Akrotiri, 10-5-71. Flt Lt R.D. Cole ejected safely. Hours flown 1304h 45m.

XP745 ff D. de Villiers 18-3-64 Samlesbury. To 56 Squadron, 20-5-65; to 29 Squadron (H), 1972. Gate guardian, RAF Boulmer, *8453M*, 1981

XP746 ff D. de Villiers 26-3-64 Samlesbury. To 56 Squadron, 15-4-65; to 111 Squadron (J), 1972.

XP747 ff T.M.S. Ferguson 8-5-64 Samlesbury. To 56 Squadron, 25-6-65. Cat 4 damage on 11-5-66, when aircraft ran off runway; repaired and returned to 29 Squadron. Crashed in sea after collision with *XP698* 16-2-72; pilot, Flt Lt Cooper, killed. Hours flown 1320h.

XP748 ff T.M.S. Ferguson 4-5-64 Samlesbury. To 56 Squadron, 4-8-65; to 11 Squadron by 12-73. Gate guardian at Binbrook, *8446M*, 1981.

XP749 ff D.M. Knight 11-12-63 Samlesbury. To the CFE, Binbrook; modified apart from large tank to F 6, 8-4-64; to 111 Squadron (K) during 1972, with 11 Group, 1981.

XP750 ff R.P. Beamont 3-1-64 Samlesbury. To the CFE, Binbrook; modified to F 6 standard, 26-3-64; to 111 Squadron (H) in 1972, 11 Group, 1981 (AQ) at Binbrook, 1983.

XP751 ff T.M.S. Ferguson 16-3-64 Samlesbury. To 74 Squadron; first full F 3 delivered for squadron service. To 111 Squadron (L) and 29 Squadron (L), 1972. With 5 Squadron (AQ) Binbrook, 1983

XP752 ff T.M.S. Ferguson 20-4-64 Samlesbury. To 74 Squadron, 1-6-64 and with 111 Squadron. Cat 5 damage after collision with French air force Mirage 111 over Colmer, 20-5-71. Used as spares and instructional airframe, *8166M*.

XP753 ff T.M.S. Ferguson 8-5-64 Samlesbury. To 74 Squadron, 23-6-64; to 29 Squadron (H), 1972. From 60 MU to 11 Squadron (L), 1973. With the LTF, Binbrook, 1983, code 'DC'. Crashed off Scarborough, 26-8-83. Pilot, Flt Lt Thompson, killed.

XP754 ff D. de Villiers 5-6-64 Samlesbury. To 74 Squadron, 31-7-64; then to 111 Squadron (R) in 1972.

XP755 ff D. de Villiers 15-6-64 Samlesbury. To 74 Squadron, 31-7-64; to 29 Squadron (E) 1972.

XP756 ff R.P. Beamont 22-6-64 Samlesbury. To 23 Squadron, 24-8-64. Crashed in sea off Great Yarmouth, 25-1-71. Capt Povilus USAF ejected safely.

XP757 ff T.M.S. Ferguson 4-7-64 Samlesbury. To 23 Squadron, 25-9-64; to 29 Squadron (M), 1972.

XP758 ff D. de Villiers 10-7-64 Samlesbury. To 23 Squadron, 14-9-64; to 111 Squadron (S), 1972.

XP759 ff D. de Villiers 14-8-64 Samlesbury. To 23 Squadron, 1-10-64; damaged after engine fire, 29-8-73, but returned to service.

XP760 ff R.P. Beamont 26-8-64 Samlesbury. To 23 Squadron, 15-10-64. Crashed in sea 24-8-66 35 nautical miles from Seahouses. Flt Lt Turley ejected safely. Hours flown 428h 5m.

XP761 ff D. de Villiers 26-8-64 Samlesbury. To 23 Squadron, 27-10-64; to 111 Squadron (N), 1972. Used in camouflage trials at Binbrook, 1981. Became *8438M*. On fire dump in 10-82.

XP762 ff D. de Villiers 3-9-64 Samlesbury. To 111 Squadron (C), 26-1-65.

XP763 ff D. de Villiers 11-9-64 Samlesbury. To 23 Squadron, 27-10-64; to 29 Squadron (P), 1972.

XP764 ff T.M.S. Ferguson 19-9-64 Samlesbury. To 74 Squadron, 3-11-64; to 29 Squadron (C), 1972; to 5 Squadron by 12-73; with the

LTF, Binbrook, 1981; 5 Squadron (AR), Binbrook, 1983.

XP765 ff D. de Villiers 26-9-64 Samlesbury. To 33 MU Lyneham, 27-11-64; to 56 Squadron (N) and 29 Squadron (A). Damaged on 5-1-68, after engaging barrier at Wattisham, repaired and returned.

XR711 ff D. de Villiers 6-10-64 Samlesbury. To 111 Squadron, 2-12-64. Destroyed at Wattisham, 29-10-71, after dropping onto runway just after take-off. Flt Lt Steenson uninjured. Aircraft removed to fire dump. Hours flown 1667h 25m.

XR712 ff D. de Villiers 12-10-64 Samlesbury. To 33 MU; to 111 Squadron (B). Crashed, 26-6-65, in sea off Padstow after display at Exeter. Flt Lt Doyle ejected safely. Hours flown 145h.

XR713 ff D. de Villiers 21-10-64 Samlesbury. To 111 Squadron (A), 8-1-65. With 5 Squadron (S) in 3-76; coded 'AR' with 5 Squadron, Binbrook, 1983.

XR714 ff D. de Villiers 14-11-64 Samlesbury. To 111 Squadron, 8-1-65. Crashed, 29-6-66, at Akrotiri during formation take-off. Repaired and returned.

XR715 ff D. de Villiers 14-11-64 Samlesbury. To 111 Squadron, 8-1-65; to 29 Squadron (R) in 1972; crashed Blyford Green, 13-2-74; remains to the RAE, Farnborough.

XR716 ff D. de Villiers 19-11-64 Samlesbury. To 111 Squadron, 4-2-65. Lightning Augmentation Flight, Binbrook, 1983; 5 Squadron (AS); 1983, inactive.

XR717 ff T.M.S. Ferguson 25-11-64 Samlesbury. To 56 Squadron, 26-3-65. In store, Boscombe Down, 8-74. Boscombe fire dump, 1981.

XR718 ff D. de Villiers 14-12-64 Samlesbury. To 56 Squadron, 1-4-65. To the BAC, Filton, 29-8-74, for storage pending disposal. 5 Squadron, Binbrook, 1983.

XR719 ff D. de Villiers 18-12-64 Samlesbury. To 56 Squadron, 16-3-65. To Shoeburyness on 9-8-66; used for instructional purposes, Coltishall, 1974.

XR720 ff J.K. Isherwood 24-12-64 Samlesbury. To 33 MU, 29-3-65; to 11 Squadron (M), 12-73; with the LTF as DA, Binbrook, 1983.

XR721 ff D. de Villiers 5-1-65 Samlesbury. To 56 Squadron, 8-4-65. Crashed on approach to Bentwaters after both engines failed, 5-1-66. Pilot, Flg Off D. Law, killed. Hours flown 220h 50m.

XR722; G27-2; 53-666 ff D. de Villiers 23-1-65 Samlesbury. Modified to full Saudi Arabian F 53 standard; used for development on SNEB bomb trials. To Saudi Arabian air base, Khamis Mushayt, 5-12-69; to No 2 Squadron, code *201*. Crashed, 6-2-72, while on loan to 6 Squadron. Capt Mohammed Saud unhurt. Hours flown 364h.

XR723 ff D. de Villiers 2-2-65 Samlesbury. To Warton as F 3, fully converted there to F 6; to 11 Squadron, 9-6-67; then to 5 Squadron (L) and 23 Squadron (K). SOC, 18-9-79.

XR724 ff D. de Villiers 10-2-65 Samlesbury. Built as F 3; converted to F 6 before despatch to 11 Squadron, 16-6-67. Inactive at Binbrook, 1983.

XR725 ff T.M.S. Ferguson 19-2-65 Samlesbury. Converted to F 6 before delivery to 74 Squadron; also with 56 Squadron (Y) in Cyprus. Inactive at Binbrook, 1983.

XR726 ff D. de Villiers 26-2-65 Samlesbury. Converted to F 6; to 60 MU, 12-7-67; to 5 Squadron (N); damaged in fire at Binbrook, 19-10-73. With the LTF(DF), 1983, at Binbrook.

XR727 ff T.M.S. Ferguson 8-3-65 Samlesbury. Converted to F 6, to 23 Squadron, 15-9-67; to 23 and 11 Squadrons. At Binbrook, 1983.

XR728 ff D. de Villiers 17-3-65 Samlesbury. Converted to F 6; to 23 Squadron, 1-11-67; to 56 and 11 Squadrons, Binbrook, 1983.

XR747 ff D. de Villiers 2-4-65 Samlesbury. Converted to F 6; to 23 Squadron, 4-1-68. At Binbrook, 1981.

XR748 ff R.P. Beamont 13-4-65 Samlesbury. Partially converted to F 6 but then 'de-modified' to F 3. First flight aborted; first flight after modification, 14-6-67. To 60 MU. Crashed 24-6-74. Pilot ejected safely.

XR749 ff T.M.S. Ferguson 30-4-65 Samlesbury. Converted to F 6 but returned to F 3 standard before delivery to 56 Squadron, 4-10-67. To 5 Squadron (Q) (BM) with 11 Squadron, Binbrook, 1983. Completely reskinned 12-82.

XR750 ff R.P. Beamont 10-5-65. Samlesbury. To 60 MU as F 3, 9-10-67.

XR751 ff J.K. Isherwood 31-5-65 Samlesbury. To 60 MU as F 3, to 5 Squadron (R), in 1973; inactive at Binbrook, 1983.

British Aircraft Corporation Ltd (Preston Division)

Lightning F 3 ER/6int Production batch, 16 built.

XR752 ff D. de Villiers 16-6-65 Samlesbury.

First interim F 6 delivered to squadron service, To the CFE, 26-11-65, to 23 Squadron (U)(C); to Warton for full F 6 modification, 20-10-67. With 11 Squadron (BH), Binbrook, 1981.

XR753 ff R.P. Beamont 23-6-65 Samlesbury. To the CFE, 16-11-65; to 5 and 23 Squadrons; to Warton for full F 6 modification, 21-3-68; to 60 MU, 18-7-69. With 5 Squadron, Binbrook, 1983.

XR754 ff D.M. Knight, 8-7-65 Samlesbury. To Boscombe Down, 3-12-65; to the AFDS, 3-66; to Warton for full F 6 modification, 31-1-67; to 23 Squadron; with 5 Squadron, Binbrook, 1983.

XR755 ff R.P. Beamont 15-7-65 Samlesbury. To 5 Squadron, 10-12-65. F 6 modification, 14-4-67; to 5 Squadron, 23-5-68; with 11 Squadron (BJ), 1983.

XR756 ff D. de Villiers 11-8-65 Samlesbury. To 5 Squadron, 10-12-65. Full F 6 modifications, 19-4-67; to 23 Squadron (M), 13-6-68. Damaged by fire, 20-8-73. At Binbrook, 1981.

XR757 ff R.P. Beamont 19-8-65 Samlesbury. To 5 Squadron, 21-12-65. Full F 6 modification, 26-1-68; to 11 Squadron (D) in 1972; with 11 Squadron (BE), Binbrook, 1983.

XR758 ff J.K. Isherwood 30-8-65 Samlesbury. To 5 Squadron (D), 11-1-66. Full F 6 modification, 16-3-67; to 11 Squadron, 24-4-68 and 74 Squadron (J). Cat 4 damage in Darwin, Australia, 11/12-69; returned to Warton, 16-1-70; re-issued to 23 Squadron, 26-4-71. To 60 MU, 26-9-73; with 5 Squadron (AF), Binbrook, 1983

XR759 ff R.P. Beamont 9-9-65 Samlesbury. To 5 Squadron (E), 18-1-66. Full F 6 modification, 18-7-67; to 60 MU, 2-8-68; to 56 Squadron (P), with 5 and 11 Squadrons, Binbrook, 1983.

XR760 ff D.M. Knight 20-9-65 Samlesbury. To 5 Squadron (J), 15-2-66; full F 6 modifications, 19-1-68; to 56 Squadron (A), Cyprus; with the LTF, Binbrook, 1981.

XR762 ff J. Carrodus 9-10-65 Samlesbury. To 5 Squadron (K), 22-2-66. Full F 6 modifications, 16-1-67; to 23 Squadron (L), 29-12-67; to 11 Squadron, 12-73.

XR763 ff T.M.S. Ferguson 15-10-65 Samlesbury. To 5 Squadron, 11-2-66. Full F 6 modification, 3-1-67. To 23 Squadron, 1-11-67; to 11 Squadron, 12-73; with 5 Squadron (AE) at Binbrook, 1983.

XR764 ff J.K. Isherwood 4-11-65 Samlesbury. To 5 Squadron (L), 1-3-66. Full F 6 modifications, 23-5-67; to 60 MU, 12-7-68; to 56 Squadron. Crashed in sea south east of Akrotiri,

30-9-71. Pilot ejected. Hours flown 937h.

XR765 ff R.P. Beamont 10-11-65 Samlesbury. To 5 Squadron (M), 8-3-66. Full F 6 modifications, 24-2-67; to 23 Squadron, 25-3-68; to 11 Squadron, 12-73; with 5 Squadron (AJ), Binbrook, 1981. Crashed into sea 30 miles east of Spurn Head, 2-7-81. Pilot ejected safely.

XR766 ff J. Dell 11-1-66 Samlesbury. To the CFE, Binbrook, 28-3-66. Crashed in sea off Leuchars east of Montrose, 7-9-67. Sqn Ldr R. Blackburn ejected safely. Hours flown 215h 15m.

XR767 ff T.M.S. Ferguson 14-1-66. Samlesbury. To the CFE, Binbrook, 5 Squadron (S) and 23 Squadron. Full F 6 modification, 29-12-67; to 5 Squadron, 24-1-69; to 74 Squadron, Tengah. Crashed into sea, 26-5-70. Pilot killed. Hours flown 680h.

British Aircraft Corporation Ltd (Preston Division)

Lightning F 6 Production batch, 39 aircraft built.

XR768 ff R.P. Beamont 24-11-65 Samlesbury. To 74 Squadron, 1-8-66; first full F 6 to be delivered. To 5 Squadron during 1973. Crashed into sea 3 miles off Mablethorpe, 29-10-74. Flt Lt Jones ejected safely. Hours flown 2120h.

XR769 ff J.K. Isherwood 1-12-65 Samlesbury. To 74 Squadron, 2-11-66. With 11 Squadron (BD), 1983.

XR770 ff R.P. Beamont 16-12-66 Samlesbury. To 74 Squadron, 26-9-66. Prior to delivery, flown on ten occasions at 1966 SBAC Display in Saudi Arabian markings. With the LAF(X), Binbrook, 1983.

XR771 ff T.M.S. Ferguson 20-1-66 Samlesbury. To 74 Squadron, 24-10-66. At Binbrook, 1981.

XR772 ff J. Dell 10-2-66 Samlesbury. To 74 Squadron, 21-10-66; to 5 Squadron (E) during 1973. Inactive at Binbrook, 1983.

XR773 ff R.P. Beamont 28-2-66 Samlesbury. To 74 Squadron, 7-11-66; to 56 Squadron (N), Cyprus. With 11 Group, 1981.

XS893 ff R.P. Beamont 15-3-66 Samlesbury. To 74 Squadron, 23-11-66. Crashed into sea off Tengah, 12-8-70. Flying Officer Rigg ejected safely. Hours flown 857h 40m.

XS894 ff R.P. Beamont 18-3-66 Samlesbury. To 5 Squadron, 3-1-67. Crashed into sea off the Wash, 5 miles north of Flamborough Head, 8-9-70. Pilot, Major Schaffer (USAF), killed. Hours flown 650h 45m.

XS895 ff R.P. Beamont 6-4-66 Samlesbury. To

74 Squadron, 5-12-66. With 5 Squadron (AK), 1983.

XS896 ff J.K. Isherwood 25-4-66 Samlesbury. To 74 Squadron, 7-12-66. Crashed on approach to Tengah, 12-9-68. Pilot, Flg Off Thompson, killed.

XS897 ff R.P. Beamont 10-5-66 Samlesbury. To 74 Squadron, 21-12-66; to 56 Squadron (S), Cyprus. Crashed 26-5-70, whilst with 74 Squadron (E). Flt Lt J. C. Webster ejected.

XS898 ff D. de Villiers 20-5-66 Samlesbury. To 5 Squadron (K), 9-1-67. With 5 Squadron (AK), Binbrook, 1983.

XS899 ff D. de Villiers 8-6-66 Samlesbury. To 5 Squadron, 23-1-67. With 5 Squadron (AA) at Binbrook, 1983.

XS900 ff R.P. Beamont 20-6-66 Samlesbury. To 5 Squadron, 31-1-67. Crashed, 24-1-68, after loss of power after take-off from Lossiemouth. Landing attempted at Milltown but failed. Flt Lt Miller ejected safely.

XS901 ff D. de Villiers 1-7-66 Samlesbury. To 5 Squadron, 20-2-67; to 56 Squadron (T), Cyprus; with 11 Squadron (BJ), 1983.

XS902 ff R.P. Beamont 14-7-66 Samlesbury. To 5 Squadron, 1-3-67. Crashed, 26-5-71, off Spurn Point. Flt Lt Mackay ejected safely. Hours flown 1051h.

XS903 ff D. de Villiers 17-8-66 Samlesbury. To 5 Squadron (A), 16-3-67; to 23 Squadron; to 5 Squadron (C); to 60 MU, 7-1-74. Inactive at Binbrook, 1983.

XS918 ff R.P. Beamont 22-9-66 Samlesbury. To 11 Squadron, 14-4-67. Crashed in sea off Leuchars 4-3-70. Pilot, Flg Off Doidge, ejected but found dead. Hours flown 874h.

XS919 ff J.K. Isherwood 28-9-66 Samlesbury. To 11 Squadron, 14-4-67; to 56 Squadron (R), Cyprus; with 5 Squadron (AD), Binbrook, 1983.

XS920 ff D. de Villiers 25-10-66 Samlesbury. To 74 Squadron, 5-12-66. To 11 Squadron (F) and 60 MU. With 11 Squadron, Binbrook, 1983, inactive.

XS921 ff D. de Villiers 17-11-66 Samlesbury. To 74 Squadron, 21-12-66; to 56 Squadron (Q), Cyprus; to 60 MU, 19-2-74. With 5 Squadron (AB), Binbrook, 1983.

XS922 ff D. de Villiers 6-12-66 Samlesbury. To 5 Squadron, 30-12-66. With 5 Squadron, Binbrook, 1983, inactive.

XS923 ff D.M. Knight 13-12-66 Samlesbury. To 5 Squadron (A), 11-1-67. With 5 and 11 Squadrons, Binbrook, 1983.

XS924 ff T.M.S. Ferguson 11-1-67 Samlesbury. To 5 Squadron, 24-2-67. Crashed, 29-4-68, during RAF 50th Anniversary display during formation take-off at Binbrook. Stalled and performed 'falling leaf' in stream turbulence. Pilot, Flt Lt Davey, killed.

XS925 ff R.P. Beamont 26-1-67 Samlesbury. To 5 Squadron, 1-3-67. Cat 4 damage, 18-11-68; returned 24-2-70 to 5 Squadron (L). With 5 Squadron (AD) at Binbrook, 1983.

XS926 ff J. Cockburn 30-1-67 Samlesbury. To 5 Squadron, 20-3-67. Crashed, 22-9-69. Spun into sea 51 miles off Flamborough Head. Major C.B. Neel USAF ejected safely. Hours flown 703h 30m.

XS927 ff R.P. Beamont 15-2-67 Samlesbury. To 74 Squadron, 3-4-67.

XS928 ff R.P. Beamont 28-2-67 Samlesbury. To 11 Squadron, 4-4-67; to 74 Squadron (L). Cat 4 damage in fire at Tengah, 6-4-70; returned to Warton by air; returned to 23 Squadron, 14-7-72; to 56 Squadron (E), Cyprus. With 11 Squadron (BJ) at Binbrook, 1983.

XS929 ff T.M.S. Ferguson 1-3-67 Samlesbury. To 11 Squadron, 26-4-67. With 11 Squadron (BC), Binbrook, 1983.

XS930 ff R.P. Beamont 20-3-67 Samlesbury. To 11 Squadron, 26-5-67. Crashed, 27-7-70, while with 74 Squadron, Tengah. Entered steep climb after take-off, looped twice and crashed into Malay village, destroying 100 buildings and injuring two villagers. Flt Lt Whitehouse killed. Hours flown 785h 55m.

XS931 ff R.P. Beamont 31-3-67 Samlesbury. To 11 Squadron (G), 31-5-67. SOC, 25-5-79.

XS932 To 11 Squadron, 21-6-67; to 56 Squadron (J), Cyprus; with the LTF, Binbrook, 1983.

XS933 ff J. Cockburn 27-4-67 Samlesbury. To 11 Squadron, 23-6-67; to 56 Squadron (K), Cyprus; at Binbrook, 1983.

XS934 ff J. Cockburn 11-5-67 Samlesbury. To 11 Squadron (K), 3-7-67. Static aircraft at Paris 1971 and Farnborough (armed as export aircraft); to 56 Squadron (B), Cyprus. Crashed in sea off Cyprus, 3-4-73. Pilot ejected safely. Hours flown 1775h 30m.

XS935 ff R.P. Beamont 29-5-67 Samlesbury. To 60 MU, 18-7-67. Inactive at Binbrook, 1983.

XS936 ff J. Cockburn 31-5-67 Samlesbury. To 60 MU, 27-7-67; to 23 Squadron. With the LTF (DF), 1983, Binbrook.

XS937 ff J. Cockburn 26-6-67 Samlesbury. To 23 Squadron, 21-8-67.

XS938 ff J. Cockburn 30-6-67 Samlesbury. To 23 Squadron (E), 28-8-67. Last production aircraft for RAF. Crashed, 28-4-71, in River Tay. Flying Officer McLean ejected safely. Hours flown 1233h 45m.

British Aircraft Corporation Ltd (Preston Division)

Lightning T 5 Production batch, 22 aircraft.

XS416 ff T.M.S. Ferguson 20-8-64 Samlesbury. To OCU Coltishall, 16-7-65; also used for 13 flights in development flying. To 11 Squadron (T). With the LTF (DU), Binbrook, 1983.

XS417 ff J. Dell 17-7-64 Samlesbury. To OCU Coltishall, 25-5-65; also used for 47 flights in development flying. First production T 5 to fly. To 23 Squadron (Z). With 11 Squadron, Binbrook, 1983.

XS418 ff T.M.S. Ferguson 12-11-64 Samlesbury. To Boscombe Down, 30-3-65; to OCU Coltishall, 7-5-65. Crashed, 23-8-68, at Stradishall, when undercarriage was retracted on landing. Flt Lt Ploseh and SAC Lewis uninjured. *8531M* at Binbrook, 1981.

XS419 ff T.M.S. Ferguson 18-12-64 Samlesbury. To OCU Coltishall, 20-4-65. Extensively damaged after hitting landing light at Coltishall in April 1965. With the LTF (DW), Binbrook, 1983.

XS420 ff D.M. Knight 23-1-65 Samlesbury. To OCU Coltishall, 29-4-65. With the LTF (DV), Binbrook, 1983.

XS421 ff T.M.S. Ferguson 25-2-65 Samlesbury. To OCU Coltishall, 11-5-65.

XS422 ff T.M.S. Ferguson 24-3-65. To OCU Coltishall, 1-6-65; to 29 Squadron, 1972; to 56 Squadron (Z), 1973. With the ETPS, Boscombe Down, 1983.

XS423 ff D. de Villiers 31-3-65 Samlesbury. To OCU Coltishall, 1-6-65. Damaged in landing accident, 17-1-68. *8532M* at Binbrook, 1981.

XS449 ff D. de Villiers 30-4-65 Samlesbury. To OCU Coltishall, 17-7-65; to 23 Squadron (T); *8533M*, at Binbrook, 1981.

XS450 ff R.P. Beamont 25-5-65 Samlesbury. To 111 Squadron, 6-9-65. *8534M*, Binbrook, 1981.

XS451 ff D. de Villiers 3-6-65 Samlesbury. To 5 Squadron, 19-11-65. Cat 3 damage at Binbrook 12-69. *8503M* at Binbrook.

XS452 ff D. de Villiers 30-6-65 Samlesbury. To OCU Coltishall, 20-9-65. With the LTF, Binbrook (inactive), 1983.

XS453 ff R.P. Beamont 6-7-65 Samlesbury. To OCU Coltishall, 10-9-65. Crashed into North Sea, 1-6-66, five miles off shore. Flying Officer Fish, on first T 5 solo, ejected safely. Hours flown 30h 30m.

XS454 ff D. de Villiers 6-7-65 Samlesbury. To RAF Leuchars on 9-10-65; returned to Warton, 5-4-68, following recurring undercarriage problems; to OCU Coltishall; Cat 3 damage, 7-3-67, when undercarriage retracted on runway. Flt Lt Graydon and Flt Lt Offord unhurt. *8535M* at Binbrook.

XS455 ff T.M.S. Ferguson 23-9-65 Samlesbury. To OCU Coltishall, 20-12-65. Crashed north of Spurn Point, 6-9-72 during aerobatic sortie. Sqn Ldr Gauvin and Lt Verist (Belgian air force) ejected but both injured. Hours flown 1085h 50m.

XS456 ff T.M.S. Ferguson 26-10-65 Samlesbury. To 56 Squadron, 20-12-65.

XS457 ff R.P. Beamont 8-11-65 Samlesbury. To OCU Coltishall, 21-12-65. At the ETPS, Boscombe Down, MoD(PE), 1981. With 11 and 5 Squadrons, Binbrook, 1983.

XS458 ff D.M. Knight 3-12-65 Samlesbury. To OCU Coltishall, 2-2-66; with 11 Squadron (BT), Binbrook, 1983.

XS459 ff J. Dell 18-12-65 Samlesbury. To OCU Coltishall; to 29 Squadron (T), used on fuel-leak-flow tests in 1972, during which the underside of the fuselage was painted white in fuel-sensitive paint. At the LTF (X), Binbrook, 1983, inactive.

XS460; 55-710 ff T.M.S. Ferguson 2-2-66 Samlesbury. Bought from the MoD by the BAC and converted to first Saudi Arabian contract T 55 export trainer. Carried out development flying at Warton. Crashed, 7-3-67, on landing at Warton, extensively damaged and SOC. J. Dell and P. Williams unhurt. Hours flown 14h 53m.

XV328 ff D. de Villiers 22-12-66 Samlesbury. To 60 MU, 31-1-67; to 29 Squadron (Z); to 5 Squadron (T) 1973. Inactive, Binbrook, 1983.

XV329 ff D. de Villiers 30-12-66 Samlesbury. To Short Bros, Belfast, for shipping to Singapore, 3-3-67. Tailplane suffered excessive damage from corrosion during voyage. (T) with 74 Squadron, Tengah.

British Aircraft Corporation Ltd (Preston Division)

Lightning T 55, Saudi Arabia Production batch, 6 aircraft.

55-711; G27-70 ff R.P. Beamont 29-8-67

Samlesbury. Front fuselage built at Filton. To Coltishall for Saudi pilot training, 2-2-68. To Saudi Arabia, 27-8-69, pilot R. Ingham, with *55-713*, for Lightning Conversion Unit at Dhahran. Damaged, 13-3-71.

55-712; G27-71 ff T.M.S. Ferguson 12-10-67 Samlesbury. Front fuselage built at Filton. Aircraft used to fly Japanese delegation (Col Yanada) at Warton, 29-11-67. To Coltishall for Saudi pilot training, 15-2-68. To Saudi Arabia, pilot R. Ingham, with *55-714*, *53-416* and *53-418*, 11-7-69. Crashed into Half Moon Bay 21-5-74 after inverted low-level pass over sand dunes. Col Ainousa and Lt Otaibi killed.

55-713; G27-72 ff R.P. Beamont 16-11-67 Samlesbury. Front fuselage built at Filton. To Coltishall for Saudi pilot training, 2-2-68. To Saudi Arabia via Akrotiri, pilot A. Love, with *55-711*. 27-8-69.

55-714; G27-73 ff R.P. Beamont and P. Millet 1-2-68 Samlesbury. Front fuselage built at Filton. To Coltishall for Saudi pilot training, 22-3-68. To Saudi via Akrotiri, pilot A. Love, with *55-712*, *53-416* and *53-418*, 11-7-69.

55-715; G27-74 ff J. Cockburn and R.T. Stock 28-2-68 Samlesbury. Front fuselage built at Filton. To Saudi Arabia, 11-3-69, pilot R. Ingham. First aircraft of T 55 batch delivered to Saudi Arabia LCU.

55-716; G27-75 ff T.M.S. Ferguson 14-7-69 Samlesbury. Front fuselage built at Filton. Replacement for *55-710* which crashed prior to delivery. To Saudi Arabia, 30-9-69, pilots J. Dell and D. Eagles.

British Aircraft Corporation Ltd (Preston Division)

Lightning T 55, Kuwait Production batch, 2 aircraft.

55-410; G27-78 ff J.L. Dell 24-5-68 Samlesbury. To Kuwait via Akrotiri and Jeddah with *53-412*, 18-12-68, pilots Sqn Ldr Caldwell and Flt Lt Pearce.

55-411; G27-79 ff J. Cockburn 3-4-69 Samlesbury. To Kuwait via Akrotiri and Jeddah with *53-423*, 3-12-69, pilots Flt Lt Adcock and Sqn Ldr Hopkins.

British Aircraft Corporation Ltd (Preston Division)

Lightning F 53, Saudi Arabia Production batch, 33 aircraft.

53-667; G27-37 ff T.M.S. Ferguson 13-7-67 Samlesbury. To Saudi Arabia, 20-9-68, pilot Flt Lt Mace; to Dhahran, 15-4-70, ex-storage;

to No 2 Squadron *202*; damaged in engine fire on ground, Dhahran, 15-4-73.

53-668; G27-38 ff R.P. Beamont 4-9-67 Samlesbury. To Saudi Arabia, 8-11-68, pilot P. Ginger, with *53-670*. To Khamis Mushayt 21-6-72. Stored before issue to No 6 Squadron.

53-669. G27-39 ff J. Cockburn 12-9-67 Samlesbury. To Jeddah, 11-10-68, pilot R. Ingham, with *53-671*. Storage at Riyadh, 1971.

53-670, G27-40 ff T.M.S. Ferguson 12-10-67 Samlesbury. To Jeddah, 8-11-68, pilot R. Ingham, with *53-668*. Storage at Riyadh, 1971.

53-671; G27-41 ff J. Cockburn 2-11-67 Samlesbury. To Jeddah, 11-10-68, pilot P. Millet. To Dhahran, 1-71, No 2 Squadron *203*, 8-70.

53-672; G27-42 ff R.P. Beamont 28-11-67 Samlesbury. Used for Kuwait demonstration on 7th flight. To Jeddah, 18-11-68, pilot R. Ingham, with *53-674*. To Dhahran, 1-70, to No 2 Squadron *204*, 7-70.

53-673; G27-43 ff R.P. Beamont 4-12-67 Samlesbury. To Jeddah, 23-8-68, pilot R. Ingham, with *53-678*. Storage at Riyadh, 9-71.

53-674; G27-44 ff T.M.S. Ferguson 12-12-67 Samlesbury. To Jeddah, 18-11-68, pilot Flt Lt Girdler, with *53-672*. To Dhahran, 22-1-70, to 2 Squadron *205*, 8-70. Crashed, 28-9-72, off coast of Bahrain. Abdul Jussef killed. Weather diversion.

53-675; G27-45 ff R.P. Beamont 19-12-67 Samlesbury. To Jeddah, 16-9-68, pilot Flt Lt Anders, with *53-679*. Storage at Riyadh, 4-71.

53-676; G27-46 ff R.P. Beamont 15-1-68 Samlesbury. To Jeddah, 20-9-68, pilot R. Ingham, with *53-667*. Storage at Riyadh, 4-71;

53-677; G27-47 ff P. Ginger 31-1-68 Samlesbury. To Jeddah, pilot P. Ginger 23-7-68, with *53-680*. Storage at Riyadh, 4-71.

53-678; G27-48 ff T.M.S. Ferguson 13-2-68 Samlesbury. To Jeddah, 23-8-68, pilot P. Millet, with *53-673*. Storage at Riyadh, 4-71.

53-679, G27-49 ff T.M.S. Ferguson 4-3-68 Samlesbury. To Jeddah, 16-9-68, pilot P. Ginger, with *53-675*, to Dhahran, 7-4-70; to 2 Squadron *206*, 8-70; loaned to 6 Squadron, 2-72; transferred to 6 Squadron, 4-72.

53-680; G27-50 ff R.P. Beamont 18-3-68 Samlesbury. To Jeddah, 23-7-68, pilot R. Ingham, with *53-677*; to Khamis Mushayt 21-6-72.

53-681; G27-57 ff R.P. Beamont 28-3-68 Samlesbury. To Jeddah, 1-7-68, pilot T.M.S. Ferguson, with *53-682*. First true export Lightning delivery. To Khamis Mushayt, 7-9-72, to 6 Squadron. This was the last Lightning flown by R. P. Beamont before retiring from test flying Lightnings.

53-682; G27-52 ff P. Millet 5-4-68 Samlesbury. To Jeddah, 1-7-68, pilot J. Cockburn, with *53-681*. To Khamis Mushayt, 7-9-72 to 6 Squadron. 'Bird-strike' in 1974, resulting in new fin being fitted,

53-683; G27-53 ff J.L. Dell 23-4-68 Samlesbury. To Saudi Arabia, 11-3-69, pilot A. Love. To Khamis Mushayt, 5-12-69; to Dhahran, 7-70. 2 Squadron *207*, 9-70.

53-684, G27-54 ff T.M.S. Ferguson 10-5-68 Samlesbury. To Jeddah, 18-11-68, pilot J. Cockburn, with *53-689*; to Dhahran, 25-1-70; to 2 Squadron *208*, 8-70.

53-685; G27-55 ff T.M.S. Ferguson 29-5-68 Samlesbury. To Saudi Arabia, 31-1-69, pilot P. Ginger, with *53-691*; to Dhahran, 16-4-70; to 2 Squadron *209*, 8-70.

53-686; G27-56; G-AWON ff T.M.S. Ferguson 11-6-68 Samlesbury. Static display at 1968 Farnborough show as improved F 53 with large stores' array and in Queen's Award markings. To Saudi Arabia, 17-4-69, pilot R. Ingham, with *53-687* and *53-688*. To Khamis Mushayt. 7-12-69; to 2 Squadron *210*, 8-70.

53-687; G27-57, G-AWOO ff P. Millet 5-7-68 Samlesbury. Flying display aircraft at 1968 Farnborough show, carried *G-AWOO* in plaque in cockpit but not externally. To Jeddah, 17-4-69, pilot D. Eagles, with *53-686* and *53-688*. To Khamis Mushayt, 7-12-69; to 2 Squadron 5-70; to LCU, 8-70.

53-688; G27-58 ff P. Ginger 12-7-68 Samlesbury. To Jeddah, 17-4-69, pilot Flt Lt Carrol, with *53-686* and *53-687*. To Khamis Mushayt, 12-69; to 6 Squadron, 3-70.

53-689; G27-59 ff P. Ginger 17-7-68 Samlesbury. To Jeddah, 18-11-68, pilot Flt Lt Craig, with *53-684*. Storage at Riyadh, 4-71.

53-690; G27-60 ff T.M.S. Ferguson 20-8-68 Samlesbury. Crashed, 4-9-68, at Pilling (Fylde) after total control failure. J. Cockburn ejected safely. Fourth flight.

53-691; G27-61 ff J. Cockburn 29-8-68 . To Jeddah, 31-1-69, pilot R. Ingham, with *53-685*. Storage at Riyadh, 4-71.

53-692; G27-62 ff J. Cockburn 24-9-68 Samlesbury. To Jeddah, 17-4-69, pilot A. Love, with *53-686, 53-687* and *53-688*. To Khamis Mushayt, 12-69; to 6 Squadron, 3-70; damaged at Khamis Mushayt, mid-1974, after engaging barrier.

53-693; G27-63 ff T.M.S. Ferguson 9-10-68 Samlesbury. To Jeddah, 23-5-69, pilot A.

Love, with *53-695, 53-415* and *53-417*. To Khamis Mushayt, 3-12-69; to 2 Squadron, 7-70; to LCU, 8-70.

53-694; G27-64 ff P. Millet 17-10-68 Samlesbury. To Jeddah, 3-6-69, pilot Flt Lt Molland, with *53-696*. To Khamis Mushayt, 3-12-69; to LCU 10-11-70. Cat 3 damage, 1-72, after engaging barrier. Flash fire, Dhahran, 18-4-73.

53-695; G27-65 ff J.L. Dell 30-10-68 Samlesbury. To Jeddah, 23-5-69, pilot R. Ingham, with *53-693, 53-415* and *53-417*. To 6 Squadron, 3-70; at Riyadh for modifications, 24-11-72.

53-696; G27-66 ff J. Cockburn 14-11-68 Samlesbury. To Jeddah, 3-6-69, pilot R. Ingham, with *53-694*. Cat 3 fire damage 9-7-69; stored until 11-70, then to LCU.

53-697; G27-67 ff D. Eagles 29-11-68 Samlesbury. To Jeddah, 26-8-69, pilot P. Millet, with *53-419*. Crashed, 3-5-70, near Yemeni border, pilot ejected, fate not known.

53-698; G27-68 ff D. Eagles 18-12-68 Samlesbury. To Jeddah, 3-6-69, pilot A. Love, with *53-699*; to Khamis Mushayt, 3-12-69; to 2 Squadron, 7-70; to LCU, 8-70.

53-699; G27-69 ff J. Cockburn 23-12-68 Samlesbury. To Jeddah, 3-6-69, pilot Flt Lt Blatchford, with *53-698*. To Khamis Mushayt, 12-69; to 6 Squadron, 3-70; to Riyadh for modification, 24-11-72.

British Aircraft Corporation Ltd (Preston Division)

Lightning F 53, Saudi Arabia Production batch, one aircraft.

53-700; G27-223 ff P. Ginger 29-6-72 Samlesbury. Last production Lightning, half-built airframe completed to replace *53-690*, which crashed before delivery. To Saudi Arabia, 4-9-72. Non-stop to Khamis Mushayt (07.30 Warton, 14.30 Khamis Mushayt). To 6 Squadron.

British Aircraft Corporation Ltd (Preston Division)

Lightning F 53, Kuwait Production batch, 12 aircraft.

53-412; G27-80 ff P. Millet 21-6-68 Samlesbury. To Jeddah, with *55-410*, 18-12-68, pilot Flt Lt Malland.

53-413; G27-81 ff T.M.S. Ferguson 13-9-68 Samlesbury. To Jeddah, 25-3-69, pilot Sqn Ldr Crumbie, with *53-414*. SOC during 1975.

53-414; G27-82 ff T.M.S. Ferguson 21-11-69 Samlesbury. To Jeddah, 25-3-69, pilot Flt Lt Brimson, with *53-413*. Crashed, 10-4-71, on approach to airfield, into shanty town, three civilians killed, pilot Razzak died on way to hospital.

53-415; G27-83 ff P. Millet 12-2-69 Samlesbury. To Jeddah, 23-5-69, pilot Capt Lopp CAF, with *53-417, 53-693* and *53-695.*

53-416; G27-84 ff D. Eagles 25-2-69 Samlesbury. To Jeddah, 11-7-69, pilot Wing Commander Blucke, with *53-418, 55-712* and *55-714.*

53-417; G27-85 ff J.L. Dell 14-3-69 Samlesbury. To Jeddah, 23-5-69, pilot Wing Commander Swart, with *53-415, 53-693* and *53-695.*

53-418; G27-86; G-AXEE ff D. Eagles 25-4-69 Samlesbury. Appeared at Paris Salon 1969 as *G-AXEE.* To Jeddah, 11-7-69, pilot Flt Lt Pengelly, with *53-416, 55-712* and *55-714.*

53-419; G27-87; G-AXFW ff P. Ginger 20-5-69 Samlesbury. To Jeddah, 26-8-69, pilot Flt Lt Fawcett, with *53-697.* Destroyed 2-8-71 at Rezayat, in take-off accident. Lt Nasser unhurt.

53-420; G27-88 ff P. Millet 8-5-69 Samlesbury. To Kuwait International Airport 19-7-69, via Akrotiri, Turkey and Iran, pilot Sqn Ldr Durham, with *53-421.* Written off in accident, details not known.

53-421; G27-89 ff P. Millet 18-6-69 Samlesbury. To Kuwait International Airport 19-7-69 via Akrotiri, Turkey and Iran, pilot Flt Lt Nicholls, with *53-420.*

53-422; G27-90 ff J. Cockburn 18-8-69 Samlesbury. To Jeddah, 4-12-69, pilot Flt Lt Bedwin, via Akrotiri.

53-423; G27-91 ff J. Cockburn 11-9-69 Samlesbury. To Jeddah, 3-12-69, pilot Flt Lt Jackson, via Akrotiri.

2   Total P 1 and Lightning production

P 1 — 2 *WG760, WG763.*

P 1B — 3 *XA847, XA853, XA856.*

— 20 Pre-production aircraft *XG307–313, XG325–337.*

F 1 — 19 *XM134–147, XM163–167.*

F 1A — 28 *XM169–192, XM213–216.*

P 11 — 2 *XL628–629.*

T 4 — 20 *XM966–974, XM987–997.*

F 2 — 44 *XN723–735, XN767–797.*

F 2A — 32 converted from airframes in the F 2 series.

F 52 — 5 converted from original batch of F 2s.

F 3 — 70 *XP693–708, XP735–765, XR711–728, XR747–751.*

F 53 — 1 of F 3 batch (*XR722*) converted to full F 53 specification.

— 33 *53-667–53-699* for Saudi Arabia.

— 12 *53-412–53-423* for Kuwait.

— 1 *53-700* Saudi Arabia to replace *53-690.*

F 3/6 Interim — 16 *XR752–767.*

F 6 — 39 *XR768–773, XS893–904, XS918–938.*

Note: 13 F 3s were also converted to F 6 standard.

T 5 — 22 *XS416–423, XS449–460, XV328–329.*

T 55 — 6 *55-711–55-716* Saudi Arabia.

— 2 *55-410–55-411* Kuwait.

Total — 339

3   Notable dates

August 4 1954 P 1, *WG760*, maiden flight, Boscombe Down.

August 11 1954 P 1 first British aircraft to exceed Mach 1 in level flight.

April 4 1957 P 1B, *XA847*, first flight from Warton.

April 3 1957 First of development batch, *XG307*, flies.

November 25 1958 First British aircraft to achieve Mach 2 (*XA847*).

October 29 1959 First F 1, *XM134*, flies.

May 14 1960 *XM135* released to the CFE.

June 29 1960 First F 1, *XM165*, to No 74 Squadron.

August 16 1960 First F 1A, *XM169*, flies.

December 4 1960 F 1A enters service with No 56 Squadron (*XM172*).

July 11 1961 First flight of Lightning F 2 (*XN723*).

November 4 1962 First F 2 to the CFE (*XN771*).

December 17 1962 F 2 enters service with No 19 Squadron (*XN775*).

June 16 1962 First flight of F 3 (*XP693*).

January 1 1964 F 3, *XP695*, to the CFE.

April 14 1964 F 3 enters service with No 74 Squadron (*XP700*).

April 17 1964 First flight of F 3 to F 6 standard (*XP697*).

16 June 1965 First flight of production F 6 (*XR752*).

November 16 1965 F 6 released to the CFE (*XR753*).

December 10 1965 F 6 enters service with No 5 Squadron.

August 25 1967 Last F 6 (*XS938*) delivered to RAF.

January 1 1968 F 2A, modified F 2, released.

January 16 1968 Last F 3 (*XR751*) to RAF.

July 22 1970 Last F 2A (*XN788*) to RAF, Germany.

4 Lightning construction and principal data

The Lightning is an all-swept, mid-wing, twin-engined, all-weather interceptor. Construction is of high-strength light alloys, with titanium panels and metal-honeycombed sandwich sections for the control-surface extremities. The controls are fully powered by duplicated hydraulic systems, driven independently from each engine and provided with spring feel, plus 'q' feel on tailplane and rudder. The hydraulically operated ailerons are hinged at a right angle to the fuselage centre-line and, on aircraft with the cambered wing, are inset from the tip. The fuselage is a parallel-section structure, housing two Rolls Royce Avon engines, with the lower unit staggered well forward of the top one; the nose intake serves both engines and has a fixed conical centre-body housing the Airpass radar. The rear fuselage carries lateral

	Span	Length	Height	Engines	Speed	Ceiling	Armament
P 1B	34' 10"	55' 3"	19' 5"	Avon 24R	M. 2.3	55,000'	2 × 30 mm Aden cannons 2 × Firestreak
F 1	34' 10"	55' 3"	19' 7"	Avon 200	M. 2.1	60,000'	4 × 30 mm Aden cannons or 2 × Firestreak plus 2 × 30 mm cannon
F 1A F 2 }	34' 10"	55' 3"	19' 7"	Avon 210	M. 2.1	60,000'	4 × 30 mm Aden cannons or 2 × Firestreak plus 2 × 30 mm cannon
T 4	as F 1 but armament reduced to Firestreak only.						
F 3	34' 10"	55' 3"	19' 7"	Avon 301	M. 2.2	60,000'+	2 × Firestreak or 2 × Red Top
T 5	as F 3 including armament.						
F 3/Interim F 6	34' 10"	55' 3"	19' 7"	Avon 301	M. 2.2	60,000'+	2 × Firestreak or 2 × Red Top plus 2 × 30 mm Aden cannons in ventral tank 24 × 2 packs of 2" rockets in place of missile pack
F 2A	As F 6 but sometimes seen with 4 × 30 mm Aden cannon armament.						
F 53	As F 6 but could also carry 2 × 1,000lb bombs, 4 SNEB Matra rocket packs and Vinten camera recce pack.						
F 55	As T 5 but with large ventral tank.						

Over-wing ferry tanks fitted to F 6 only, although some F 3s were to be seen flying with mock-ups during F 6 development. Finlets originally fitted to over-wing tanks were found to be unnecessary.

All aircraft apart from F 1 were fitted with in-flight refuelling capability.

All aircraft were fitted with Martin-Baker Type BS4 seats and their derivatives, with 90 kts capacity.

*Much information is still classified, the above is listed as a guide only.

hydraulically operated airbrakes, located high on the fuselage just forward of the fin leading edge. The single-piece, all-moving tailplane is set low to alleviate pitch-up tendencies and its outline shape approximates that of the wing. Cockpit equipment includes a Martin-Baker Type 4 ejection seat, a pilot attack sight for the Airpass system and the AI radar scope, plus a roller-blind horizon and Flight Director. The main undercarriage is fitted with Maxaret anti-skid units and multi-cylinder disc brakes; an Irving ring-slot parachute is also provided, in the rear fuselage, for braking purposes.

Typical equipment for F 6 and export derivatives

Engines	Avon 300 series with 11,100 lb thrust cold, 16,300 lb reheat
Fuel pumps	Two type GBB131, two FBP104/111 (boosters) and two TPE101 (transfer)
Fuel capacity	10,600 lb internally, including ventral tank plus 4,320 lb in over-wing ferry tanks
Fuel type	Avtur 50 or Avtag
Ejection seat	Martin-Baker BS4C Mk 2
Oxygen	3.5 litre capacity, liquid oxygen system
Fire control	Graviner automatic zone-warning system, pilot-initiated selective extinguishing
Radar and fire control system	Ferranti type AI23S including: approach and attack computers; search and display attack unit; radar control and mode-selector switch, visual display cine-recorder
Flight control system	Integrated flight-instrumentation display, type OR946 phase 2; Airdata system Mk 2 navigation display unit; master reference gyro, ILS
Navigation aids	Compass; remote magnetic flux detector updates master gyro TACAN, with offset computer. UHF Homing; IFF Mk 10 with SIF (Radio Compass Special Ferry Fit)
Standby instruments	Artificial horizon Type 6H; directional gyro indicator Type B; Compass type E2B; altimeter Mk 26, ASI Mk 18
Radio	Multi-channel UHF/VHF transmitter/receiver. UHF stand-by set with two communications' channels
Hydraulics	Two type 180 Mk 50/65 services, two type 220 Mk 37 controls, 3,000 psi for systems and 1,500 psi for brakes
Electrics	Engine air, turbine-driven alternator, 200V 3-phase 400 Hz. Engine air, turbine-driven generator 28.5V DC and back-up stand-by generator supply battery 24V DC.

Index